Muscle Building

This Guide to Isometric Exercises for Muscle Building

(A Life Changing Strength Training Guide for the Best Body in Your 40s and Beyond)

Julius Penaflor

Published By **Regina Loviusher**

Julius Penaflor

All Rights Reserved

Muscle Building: This Guide to Isometric Exercises for Muscle Building (A Life Changing Strength Training Guide for the Best Body in Your 40s and Beyond)

ISBN 978-1-9992123-4-6

No part of this guidebook shall be reproduced in any form without permission in writing from the publisher except in the case of brief quotations embodied in critical articles or reviews.

Legal & Disclaimer

The information contained in this book is not designed to replace or take the place of any form of medicine or professional medical advice. The information in this book has been provided for educational & entertainment purposes only.

The information contained in this book has been compiled from sources deemed reliable, and it is accurate to the best of the Author's knowledge; however, the Author cannot guarantee its accuracy and validity and cannot be held liable for any errors or omissions. Changes are periodically made to this book. You must consult your doctor or get professional medical advice before using any of the suggested remedies, techniques, or information in this book.

Upon using the information contained in this book, you agree to hold harmless the Author from and against any damages, costs, and expenses, including any legal fees potentially resulting from the application of any of the information provided by this guide. This disclaimer applies to any damages or injury caused by the use and application, whether directly or indirectly, of any advice or information presented, whether for breach of contract, tort, negligence, personal injury, criminal intent, or under any other cause of action.

You agree to accept all risks of using the information presented inside this book. You need to consult a professional medical practitioner in order to ensure you are both able and healthy enough to participate in this program.

Table Of Contents

Chapter 1: Mindset For Muscle

More than 90% of men who were given right down to collect muscle fail. They pull themselves to the health club, do the equal worn-out exercising, down their protein drink, troll the muscle boards – and end up looking just like the equal weedy dreamer that they started out out being. Out of frustration, they may turn out to be making an investment in a program like this one. But, then they'll straight away skip to the exercising section. After all, that's the meaty element, right. Building muscle is about throwing weight around, not indulging in mindless psycho-babble.

Those men will in no way collect a extremely good physique. In fact, they'll spend the relaxation in their workout lives spinning their wheels. Until they – till you – recognize that they key to muscle growth has not some thing to do with operating out, or perhaps consuming right, they'll be incessantly condemned to bodybuilding purgatory. The easy fact is that 90% of building muscle is prepared what is going among your ears. Why do you believe you studied that Arnold modified into able to emerge as the excellent bodybuilder on this planet at the same time as many men who skilled proper together with him, the use of the same, if not greater, weight, you've by no means heard of? The purpose is that Arnold changed into a grasp at self motivation, visualization and purpose setting.

To attain achievement at constructing muscle, you want to take a leaf out of the e book of professional athletes who deal with their exercising exercises like a battlefield venture. If you want to get the maximum from your education effort, you need to apply laser like popularity to each element of your exercising. In reality, you ought to divide your highbrow training reputation into 2 factors:

Before the Workout

During the Workout

Before the Workout

(1) Mentally rehearse the exercise within the hour earlier than you hit the gym. See yourself grabbing the weights and powering via the ones final 3 tough reps. Focus to your without delay goal, this is to do extra than you probable did in your final workout - an extra rep, any other 2 kilos of weight or a discounted rest among gadgets. Do this for every workout.

(2) Discuss your unique exercising plans for that day together with your friends. Tell them you are surely focused on getting eight reps with 30 pound dumbbells on the bench press. Put it available.

(three) Surround yourself with notable human beings. Remember . . .

If you lay with puppies, you'll upward thrust up with fleas.

Actively are searching for out people who will assist you. They will pull you up even as you need it and enhance your every day desires.

(four) Be distracted early. When you first stroll into the gym, pause to take in the surroundings. Check out who's there and what's specific. Doing this early allows you no longer to be distracted whilst you flick the transfer and your exercising begins offevolved.

(five) Build up your inner electricity. An hour earlier than your exercising, your engine have to be idling at a 4. By the time you stroll into the gymnasium it want to be as a outstanding deal as a 7. During your heat-up, it's reached 8.Five. And by the time you pile the burden on for your first set, you're hitting 10.

During the Workout

(1) Focus straight away at the taking walks muscle group. Get related. If you are doing barbell curls, located your thoughts into your biceps. Let no longer whatever else don't forget. That way you'll be capable of honestly interact a muscle and recruit as many muscle fibers as possible.

(2) Switch off your mind. At least the part of it that is bent on sabotaging your exercise. You understand the element. It's continuously looking for to rationalize with you to get you to do an awful lot less. So you don't injure yourself. So you don't run out of time. So you don't over-educate. Don't negotiate with this facet of your thoughts. Instead, tell your thoughts that what you're doing is easy. Don't popularity at the weight that you're lifting. Visualize your body as a system, your legs and arms as pistons, mechanically using the weight up and down.

(3) Play thoughts video video games on yourself. This is a manner that expert athletes were the usage of for decades to offer almost superhuman outcomes from their paintings-outs. Tom Platz is a legend among bodybuilders for his extremely good leg improvement. His paintings-outs were the epitome of depth. Here's how he'd collect it:

Platz need to continuously play highbrow suggestions on himself all through a set.

While doing a set of squats, as an example, he might possibly persuade himself that his wife had been kidnapped and that a person emerge as keeping a gun to her head. Unless he completed the proscribed sort of reps, she may be useless.

Can you bear in mind the depth that you may generate if that changed into your truth? Well, it is able to be. Here are some awesome highbrow suggestions that you can play on your self in case you want to demand more from your self within the course of those very last difficult reps:

(1) Tell your self that a millionaire has really supplied you $1 million to get that subsequent rep.

(2) Picture an imaginary spotter who is popularity over you, helping you to eke out that remaining rep.

(3) Imagine that an explosion has honestly befell within the part of your frame which you're working. Let the energy of the blast

explode you through that final rep (clearly don't sacrifice shape in this one).

(4) Insult yourself. Sometimes a bit little little bit of strategic terrible self communicate can artwork wonders. There's a traditional scene in Pumping Iron in which Arnold Schwarzenegger is spotting Franco Columbu on a difficult and rapid of bench presses. Franco receives the burden caught on his chest and, in place of helping him, Arnold calls him a 'lazy bastard.' Franco then grits his enamel and powers the weight all over again up. You don't need Arnold spherical. Call yourself a lazy bastard.

(five) Make it a life or loss of life revel in. Picture yourself eliminating a cliff by means of way of your fingertips. If you may't get that weight up, then your grip goes to fail and it'll all be over.

Chapter 2: Eating To Get Huge

Most humans don't understand how loads meals you need to eat to gain natural muscle mass. Eating might also sound like masses of amusing, however continuously getting the clean substances of muscle building nutrients into your machine within the portions on the manner to make a difference is tough, to mention the least. Unless, you provide your body with the building blocks of muscle food, you could by no means build a pleasing frame.

Your purpose with consuming over the subsequent one year is probably to advantage muscular length. Despite the advertising and advertising that we see all around us approximately how you may get ripped on the equal time as packing on mass, that isn't always what you're after right now. You can't realistically get six % abs at the identical time as setting a dozen pounds of muscle mass onto your frame.

To gain muscle businesses, you need to educate hard and clever. You moreover want to offer your frame the time to get higher, top off and rebuild. The zero.33 component is fuel, inside the form of vitamins. If you are taking in extra fine strength than you're burning, then the stability can be carried out to assemble muscle corporations.

This doesn't advise that you are going to throw your self into the vintage faculty bulking up mentality. Clearly all energy are not identical. Gaining weight is not your purpose right here – gaining lean muscle mass is what that is all approximately. That's why you'll be ingesting smooth nearly all the time.

Neither will you're taking pride in a unmarried the cutting-edge crop of fad diets that are promulgating our on-line world proper now. Intermittent fasting, the Keto weight loss plan or some thing else that hits your inbox may match for some. But for you, right now it certainly doesn't study. You are going to stay with a essential balanced, macronutrient software program based totally on electricity regular with day.

Your Maintenance Calorie Level

In order to determine how many strength you need to be consuming every day, you want to first of all exercise consultation how many electricity you want to be taking in simplest to characteristic. Everything you do , from respiration to scratching your nostril, burns energy. If you don't take in sufficient calories to meet these dreams, then you may find out your self in a catabolic state (not a fantastic area to be).

A easy components to can help you exercise your preservation calorie diploma is to multiply your modern-day body weight in kilograms by using 24.

Alternatively, multiply your modern-day frame weight in pounds with the aid of way of zero.Forty 5, then through way of 24

Let's take a a hundred 80 pound man. First we'll multiply his body weight via 0.Forty five to get his weight in kilograms . . .

one hundred and eighty x 0.Forty 5 = 81 kilograms

Now, we do the second one calculation . . .

eighty one x 24 = 1944

So, we now understand that our 100 eighty pound man calls for about 1950 electricity regular with day to keep his contemporary bodyweight and deliver the electricity for his sports over a 24 hour duration.

Our purpose, of path, is not to hold our body weight. We want to feature muscle mass. We don't want to feature too many power, as we're aware of putting on lean mass most effective. A practical quantity to shoot for is 500 greater electricity in keeping with day. 500 energy is attainable, with out leaving your enjoy bloated. Yet, over the route of one year (and also you need to be taking into consideration this as a yearlong software program application), you may have taken in a further 178,000 power. This will offer your frame with a whole of exquisite fuel for building muscle.

So, allow's cross back to our one hundred and eighty pound guy, and upload our greater calorie bear in thoughts . . .

1944 + 3 hundred = 2444

We now have our each day calorie rely variety of round 2450 energy steady with day.

Now, in reality, you aren't going to take all of these strength into your body in a single large meal. But, neither need to you achieve this over the route of 3 food. To provide prime gas in your body you need to present it a persistent deliver of nutrients. In truth you need to be feeding it every and a half of hours. So, that is what you'll be doing. You'll have a look at greater about why and how your have to be consuming each two-3 hours in Chapter Six, however for now you want to set up what number of strength you have to be ingesting at every meal.

To do that, we simply divide your usual calorie discern through six.

So, for our 100 and eighty pound man . . .

2450 / 6 = 408 power

Our a hundred eighty pound guy desires to be ingesting 408 calories every meal, with food spaced 3 hours aside.

Macronutrient Breakdown

The 3 macro-vitamins in our components are proteins, carbohydrates and fats. Well take a look at them in greater element inside the next financial disaster. Our way right now might be to installation the proper ratio between the ones food for every of your six food.

Carbohydrates are the power deliver that your body is predicated upon for the whole thing that it does. Carbs are specifically vital for those, such as you, who are engaged in hard, excessive weight resistance education.

Protein, of direction, is essential for building muscle. Everything to your body consists of amino acids, the constructing blocks of protein. In order to get over your sports activities and rebuild your frame, you need to ensure that a steady deliver of first-rate protein is flowing via your blood circulate.

Fats are available in suitable and awful types. The appropriate fat are referred to as crucial fatty acids (EFA's). The primary training of EFA's are omega-three and omega-6. You want them for an entire host of fitness, fitness and muscle constructing benefits. The extremely good property are fatty fish like salmon, sardines herring, mackerel and rainbow trout further to flaxseeds, walnuts, fish oil, avocado and flaxseed oil.

The perfect macronutrient for the mass gaining bodybuilder is . . .

50% Carbs / 30% Protein / 20% Fats

That manner that, at every meal, half of of your plate have to be full of complicated and fibrous carbs, 3 fifths of the opportunity half of of need to embody a remarkable lean protein and the stability ought to be a wholesome fats.

Nutrition Guidelines Summary

☐ Have your first meal even as you first stand up within the morning, then place them out every and a half hours, i.E. . .

7am

9:30am

12pm

2:30pm

5:00pm

7:30pm

Don't bypass food – art work the plan. In the following chapter, you'll find out some super thoughts on how you could ensure that you get in very unmarried meal, even while you're on the go!

Cut out calorie laden drinks. Stick with water.

Make practical use of liquid protein dietary supplements. They are amazing way that will help you get your protein and strength while you're on the run. Don't have more than meals ordinary with day inside the shape of protein shakes, however.

Count energy for the primary couple of weeks. From there you have got so as to gauge your meal sizes through sight.

Allow your self one cheat meal each seven days. Make it a noon meal if feasible. Enjoy yourself, but don't skip too crazy!

Make positive that your post workout meal lets in you to get terrific protein and carbs into your body inner twenty mins of completing the workout.

Chapter 3: Training For Real Muscle Mass

The key to building and retaining regular muscle tissues is range. The terrific software program in the global for you may provide you with effects for most effective goodbye. That's due to the reality our our our our bodies are rather adaptive. When they come to be acclimatized to a exercise software, your consequences will lessen – and subsequently prevent all together. That is why you'll provided with exercise levels in this e-book:

Phase One: Foundational Mass Training

Phase Two: Peripheral Heart Action Training

Your 12 Month Training Plan

You may be alternating between those workout structures over the direction of the following 12 months. Begin collectively with your Phase One Program. Stick with it for eight weeks, that specialize in getting more potent at the identical time as maintaining first-rate shape. At the cease of 8 weeks, take a complete week off from schooling. Then go into your Phase Two Program. Work this program for a further 8 weeks. Then take some other whole week off. Now waft lower again on your Phase One Program for a further 8 weeks.

This Phase One / Phase Two rotation with consistent with week's hole among every segment will will let you whole three tiers of every exercise over the following 365 days.

Phase One: Foundational Mass Training

The bodybuilding magazines and net web sites have made building muscle highly complicated (and fantastically worthwhile) to the quantity that each man thinks he wishes to do at least 6 exercising for his biceps and triceps on my own. Split sporting events are the default exercising fashion. Anything lots much less is for the pencil neck geek and the clueless klutz.

Let every person else inside the gym hold on their merry multi exercising, isolation focused way. You are going to educate smarter. For a difficult gainer to assemble muscle what's desired is developing the weights, losing the reps, taking longer rest durations between units and to reputation at the simple compound wearing sports. That's why your entire habitual is going to include the large 6 mass builders . . .

Squats

Dead-lifts

Pull Ups

Bench Press

Military Press

That's it! No barbell curls, no p.C dec flyes, no lying leg curls. Put all your energy and attention into the compound sporting events which might be already running every muscle on your body.

What's more, you'll only be inside the gym times every week. Go with Monday and Thursday, to provide most relaxation between bodily games. Do not be tempted to do extra exercising than this - it's far going to be counterproductive. Just make certain that each single 2d of every workout is complete on.

From now on, your education mindset wants to be: Get in, art work your body like hell, then get out.

Unless you get your choice of exercise right, you're going to be dropping pretty a few time inside the gymnasium for little or no praise. Heavy compound moves are the vital issue to building muscle companies. These are the multi-joint moves that artwork a number of muscle organizations simultaneously. They moreover simulate actual existence moves, like squatting down or lifting some factor off the ground. Prime examples of compound moves are chin ups, squats and the bench press. These carrying occasions are not only the remarkable manner to construct bulk and they will get you stronger faster than some component else. And, due to the fact they art work muscle agencies concurrently, they are some distance more time green than isolation moves.

Optimized Exercise Technique

The following bodily games will shape the basis of your training:

Squats

Dead-lifts

Pull Ups

Bench Press

Military Press

Let's now take a close study each of those middle sports:

SQUATS

Squats are called a compound exercising, meaning that they purpose a couple of muscle organization. This clean motion does, in truth, right away stimulate each muscle organization inside the lower frame. The excessive movers, but, are the inner thighs, the butt and the hips. Indirectly, the squat even gives a exercise to the muscular tissues of the pinnacle frame. It moreover generates a exquisite cardiovascular advantage. By taking deep breaths among every repetition and forcing the air out of the frame at the ascent, the coronary heart and lungs can be walking more time to manual the artwork of the muscular tissues of the body. This ensures that a ton of power are being burnt and that the cardiovascular gadget is getting a rev up at the same time.

Preparation: Place an Olympic bar on the squat rack. At a weight of forty five lbs you won't want to feature any introduced weight however make certain that use a pad in the center of the bar to defend your neck.

Execution: Position your self below the bar and raise it off the rack. Step again and stand together collectively with your toes spread slightly wider than shoulder width and pointing slightly outward. Keep your once more right now, your chest thrust out and your head up. Now stressful your belly wall, bend your knees and decrease your body until your thighs are parallel with the ground. To keep away from more strain on the knees, don't bypass down any in addition. While squatting, preserve your head up and your decrease again slightly arched.

In the bottom squat position, your decrease legs need to be nearly vertical to the ground. Push thru your heels as you return to the start feature.

Breathing: Because squats encompass an cardio element, it's vital that you use right respiratory method. If you don't you can start to sense mild headed after some repetitions. As you lower yourself, breathe in deeply. Then at the way again up, forcefully expel the air in a single breath. During the very last few repetitions, take or 3 quick breaths between reps.

What Not To Do When You Squat

Squatting over a bench. Every time you touch the bench collectively together with your glutes, your backbone will compress barely. Over time this can motive vertebral damage.

Placing a block below your heels / turning your toes too extensively outwards. Both of those will location unnatural stresses to your knees and, over time, can cause damage.

Leaning too a ways beforehand. Not most effective does this growth your chance of suffering spinal accidents, it additionally takes the stress off the quadriceps and onto the trunk extensor muscular tissues.

Allowing the knees to experience over the feet whilst allowing your heels to raise off the ground. Keeping your decrease legs nearly vertical may additionally moreover moreover enjoy unnatural on the start but it may make the difference among injured and healthful knees. Keeping your shin bones vertical considerably reduces your threat of damage.

DEAD-LIFTS

Often known as the king of wearing sports, the barbell deadlift is a completely powerful mass builder. It especially targets the legs and again, but will region secondary adaptive stress upon almost each muscle employer to your body. Here's a way to perform them efficiently:

Squat down so your toes are beneath the bar, and the bar rests in the direction of your shins. Grip the bar using an trade hook grip to prevent it from rotating. Your hands should be a touch wider than shoulder width apart. Make sure to hold your lower back flat and tight at some level within the movement.

Begin lifting the bar with an extended, sturdy leg push, extending your knees and hips. Your knees have to be bent as you growth the bar past them. Pull your shoulder blades collectively as you do this. Push your hips in closer to the bar and maintain the bar near your frame at some point of the enhance.

Continue the elevate as if pushing the ground away from you at the aspect of your feet, besides you rise up immediately collectively collectively with your knees locked. Brace your shoulders lower decrease back as you enhance. Also ensure that you grip the bar tightly, just so it doesn't rotate on your hand.

With your knees unlocked, and maintaining a respectable, flat again and keep your head up, begin to decrease the bar below control. Your knees ought to be bent as you decrease the bar past them. Move your hips once more and down as you descend.

Slowly circulate your hips and shoulder collectively while reducing the bar backpedal to the begin feature. Do not drop the bar. Make effective which you are bending on the knees and pulling your shoulders back.

Correct lifting approach is essential with this movement. Never boom together along side your spine flexed ahead. Not most effective will the exercise be vain if you do, but you moreover mght risk spinal damage. Always beautify and reduce your shoulders and hips together. Keep the bar close to your body and do not drop it at the stop of the movement. Always lower the bar beneath manipulate.

Dumbbell Variation

Using dumbbells for the deadlift recruits greater muscles to manipulate and stabilize motion. It is a extremely good way of growing power and method for heavier barbell lifts. Start with moderate weights to determine your shape of movement. As with the barbell increase, hold your decrease returned flat and the weights close to your frame. Do now not pause at the lowest of the movement or permit the weights to 'jump' as you lower them.

WIDE GRIP PULL UPS

Wide Grip Pull Ups to the the the front are a splendid movement to widen the higher once more and create a full sweep inside the lats. Chinning yourself so that you contact the chest to the bar instead of the back of the neck gives you a barely longer sort of movement and is an awful lot a good deal much less strict, permitting you to cheat barely so you can hold your reps even at the same time as you are worn-out.

Method:

(1)   Take hold of the chinning bar with an overhand grip, fingers as large apart as practicable.

(2)   Hang from the bar, then pull yourself up, looking for to the touch the pinnacle of your chest to the bar. At the top of the movement, maintain for a fast 2d, then decrease yourself once more to the beginning role.

Tips for Maximum Results

Pay hobby to the data so that you can extract the most from the motion. Let your legs hold down proper away, and don't jerk your manner up. Just pull your self up in a clean movement, then allow your body down beneath control. Jerking movements shift the strive, taking anxiety off the lats.

For most stretch and contraction, decrease yourself to the very backside of each rep and pull up till the bar touches the chest (or your chin within the later reps of the set).

A grip sincerely out of doors the shoulders can be very powerful. However, you need to variety it to stimulate the muscle pretty differently. The vast grip invitations the tendency to do half reps, but higher improvement comes with complete range ones.

As you bypass your grip at the pull up bar closer to your midline, the extra the decrease lat development together with the intercostals. Try a sequence of sets, starting with and completing slim, inching your grip closer with the set.

Shoot for a selected quantity of reps, say 50, instead of counting devices. On the primary set you can do 10 reps. Perhaps you warfare with 8 on the second set. You've now were given 18 reps. If you are making 5 on the 1/three set, you're as a great deal as 23 reps.

Continue to characteristic them till you have had been given reached 50, despite the fact that it could take you 20 gadgets to do it. That will will can help you construct every length and strength.

After you've mastered 10-12 reps in any form of pull up, you may begin to positioned weight round your waist. That's at the same time as the muscle certainly begins offevolved to broaden. Add approximately ten pounds at a time, which must make the reps tougher. As you grow to be stronger, ad more weight. It's pleasant whilst you're capable of start including weight that your final will truly amplify!

BENCH PRESS

The flat barbell bench press is the number one compound mass builder for the higher frame. By setting you in a function of strength, the motion allows you to raise very heavy weight, and so place maximal pressure on your muscle tissues. The number one mover for the bench is the %, but it will provide an superb exercising to your triceps, shoulders and lats.

Most guys, however, misuse this key exercise. So permit's make clean some aspect proper right here – you'll be the usage of the bench press as a device to assist you to gather muscle tissues. It is not approximately lifting as an entire lot weight as viable. You aren't schooling to be a powerlifter. That way leaving your ego at the door and the usage of accurate bodybuilding form to maximally stimulate the muscle groups of your chest.

Basic bench press method

(1)   Position your self at the bench together with your feet resting fats on the ground and your shoulders in line with the uprights. Your head ought to be supported by using manner of way of the bench generally.

(2)   Grasp the bar at a piece past shoulder width overhand grip.

(three)   Un-rack the load and resource it at hands period in step with your collar bone.

(4)   To bring the burden down pull your shoulder blades collectively. The bar need to come back on your decrease chest.

(five)   Press the weight up in an arcing motion, preserving your shoulder blades pulled in continuously – don't lock out on the top.

Here's the way to optimize that approach:

☐ Put your feet up on the bench. This will do topics to make your chest art work extra tough:

(1) Take your quads out of the exercising

(2) Cut out returned arch in the path of the energy upwards

☐ Reposition your grip in order that your forearms a touch plenty less than parallel then un-rack the weight. In the absolutely extended feature, pinch collectively the shoulder blades.

☐ Rather than decrease to chest, deliver the bar all of the manner right down to your sternum, which is proper away under the chest.

☐ In the bottom feature, make an exaggerated stretch of your percentage, then right away energy the load once more up. Make sure to maintain the shoulders down as you push up.

MILITARY PRESS

The military press is the granddaddy of all shoulder carrying activities. It immediately hits the the the front and side deltoids, to present you each shoulder width and thickness. When you do the motion from a seated characteristic the motion can be stricter than on the equal time as recognition.

Basic Military Press approach:

(1) From a sitting function, draw close to a barbell with an overhand grip and maintain it at shoulder stage, pams under for support, arms out of doors your shoulders, elbows tucked in and beneath.

(2)   From a characteristic about even together with your collarbone, boost the bar right now up overhead until your palms are locked out, being careful to preserve the burden balanced and under manipulate. Lower the burden decrease returned to the start characteristic.

Optimized Military Press technique:

From the bottom characteristic, pass your elbows ahead honestly so they may be absolutely in the front of your torso, in preference to flared again. This will take the focus of pressure from your pinnacle back and vicinity it for your delts. This can even relieve masses of the tension out of your spine. This may require you to drop again the load barely. The higher delt attention, but, will more than compensate.

Extra Tips:

Use a extensive grip (too slim a grip shifts the point of interest to the triceps)

Do not lock out on the top of the movement

Keep your again arched at some point of

Do now not soar the burden off your chest

The Workout

Now that you've were given to grips with the right widespread universal overall performance of every of the sports on your again to foundational mass training exercise, allow's test a way to located them together to ensure most consequences. Remember which you'll be on foot the entire body in every session and education twice in line with week. The satisfactory education days will allow for as a minimum entire rest days amongst them.

Rep & Set Scheme

For every exercising, except for pull ups, use the subsequent rep scheme:

Warm Up – 15 reps

Working units – 12 reps

10 reps

eight reps 6 reps

For Pull Ups, set your self a cause of 30 reps within the first two weeks. Do that is as few sets as feasible, as defined in the Pull Ups workout description. After weeks, up the reason to forty reps. After more weeks, increase it another time to 50 reps.

Both research and revel in have verified that bodybuilders get the maximum muscle constructing advantage from schooling with a weight that is among 70 and 75 percentage in their one rep most. Your one rep max is the amount of weight that you could elevate at the same time as doing one complete-out rep with perfect form. When you pyramid your reps, as you will be doing, you slightly boom the load as you lower the reps.

The weight which you select want to intend that you are schooling to failure on every set. This way that you'll be continuing the set till you could't do any more reps with that weight without stopping to relaxation.

You'll be doing four running devices on each exercising (apart from pull ups, as a manner to take as many gadgets as required to hit your intention). You need to do as a minimum four units which will have the extent of education important to absolutely stimulate all of the available muscle. If you do extra sets consistent with workout, your widespread training quantity might be so first rate which you chance over training.

WORKOUT A: FOUNDATIONAL MASS TRAINING

EXERCISE   REPS

Squats   15 – 12 / 10 / eight / 6

Deadlift   15 – 12 / 10 / 8 / 6

Pull Ups   Total 30 reps

Bench Press   15 – 12 / 10 / eight / 6

Military Press   15 – 12 / 10 / 8 / 6

How Long?

You ought to preserve in this schooling software program program for 8 weeks. That might be extended enough on the way to need to three actual improvement in your energy and muscle profits, but now not too prolonged to result in diminishing returns due to over familiarization.

At the quit of eight weeks, take a whole week off from training earlier than stepping into your Phase Two software program.

Phase Two: Peripheral Heart Action Training

Peripheral Heart Action Training has been spherical due to the fact the 1940's, even as it become superior with the aid of Dr Arthur Steinhaus. It have become popularized inside the '60's through way of manner of Mr. Universe identify holder Bob Gajda. PHA is designed to keep the blood circulating throughout the whole body at a few degree in the exercising. Even no matter the truth that it can sound like circuit training, it's far without a doubt a completely immoderate and a very powerful manner to p.C. Muscles onto your frame. Unlike circuit training, PHA calls for that you use heavy weight and which you stay with nicely shape.

This is a top notch workout alternative for hard gainers. PHA training will supply your muscle groups an exceptional pump. By shunting the blood at some stage in the body, you'll moreover be receiving some critical neuromuscular results. The numerous rep and goal muscle scheme creates extra neurological pathways to the strolling muscle. This will increase blood go together with the drift to the muscle.

PHA schooling is constructed round compound movements – much like those you've been using eventually of your Phase One training. A crucial reason of your exercising may be to shunt the blood spherical your body. Because you may be doing consecutive gadgets for considered one in all a kind body components, you may be allowing the purpose muscle greater relaxation than with conventional schooling.

This will will assist you to use neat maximal power output on each and every set.

With PHA schooling you need to be that specialize in making your workout greater excessive with each and every session. Here's the way to do this:

push out extra reps with the identical weight

do greater sequences within the same time location

positioned greater weight on the bar

Performing PHA training with essential, compound multi-joint carrying occasions like squats, deadlifts, and overhead presses may be fantastically tough art work. In reality, the purpose that PHA training isn't used more often is in fact that it's far too damned tough for optimum human beings an amazing manner to attend to for any time period. But you're no longer maximum humans – right?

How Does PHA Work?

Peripheral Heart Action training involves doing tri-sets of sports. This method that you do one set of an workout, then bypass immediately to each other exercise for a special body issue, accompanied via way of way of a totally ultimate workout for a third frame issue. After a rest duration, you flow on in your subsequent tri-set. The workout commonly consists of or 3 of these tri sets to art work the whole body.

In this software you'll be finishing three devices of tri sets in keeping with exercise. This is excessive education, as you pass right far from one exercise to the subsequent with none rest. At the give up of your tri set, you relaxation for two to a few mins earlier than you circulate in your subsequent set.

You could be education every extraordinary day in this application. Remember that the bodily video games which are grouped together on your tri set isn't always for the same body element. You may be each acting

Workout 1 or Workout 2, alternating them each workout.

The PHA Rep Scheme

A precise trouble of the PHA System which you are approximately to embark upon is the tailored rep scheme. Each workout in a tri set has its very own rep remember variety. Here's the way it definitely works:

Exercise One: The first workout that you may do in each tri set can be achieved for five reps. That manner that you will be the usage of a completely heavy weight on that movement. You want to not visit failure, but.

Exercise Two: The second workout can be finished for a rep depend of among 8 and 12. Start with a weight with a purpose to permit eight unique reps. As you get more potent, boom the reps till you could do 12. At that point growth the load to the extent which you are yet again simplest able to pump out 8 reps.

Exercise Three: The 0.33 exercising in your tri set will comprise doing amongst 15 and 20 reps. This will gorge the muscle with blood, offering an tremendous pump.

WORKOUT B: PERIPHERAL HEART ACTION (PHA)

WORKOUT 1

TRI-SET A

SQUATS   three X five-eight

DUMBBELL INCLINE PRESS   3 X 8-12

UPRIGHT ROWING   3 X 15-20

TRI-SET B

PULL UPS   three X five-eight

DUMBBELL CURLS   3 X 8-12

FLYES   3 X 15-20

NOTE: Always perform a slight warmth-up set at the number one motion of every tri-set.

WORKOUT 2

TRI-SET A

DEADLIFT   three X five-8

CALF RAISES   3 X 8-12

SIDE LATERAL RAISES   3 X 15-20

TRI-SET B

DUMBBELL SHOULDER PRESS   three X five-8

LUNGES   three X 8-12

TRICEP PUSHDOWNS   3 X 15-20

The Exercises

Some of the bodily sports activities that you may be the usage of for your PHA schooling segment are familiar to you out of your Phase One software. In this section we define the right method for those who are not.

Dumbbell Incline Press

If the incline bench you are using is adjustable, set it to a completely steep thoughts-set (no extra than 30 levels from vertical). The steep perspective focuses the exercise on the uppermost phase of the %. Bring the dumbbells up on your chest stage. In the beginning characteristic the weights need to be resting in competition in your shoulders.

Press the dumbbells up, using the p.C. To drag the arm up and skip the chest. Following this direction makes the exercising extra robust and locations minimal emphasis at the primary synergist, the triceps. Keep your another time flat in opposition to the bench as you increase.

At the top of the movement, stoop your shoulders in advance and as an awful lot as unsure which you get whole percent stimulation. Lower the dumbbells yet again to the region to begin. At the lowest of the motion, revel in for a stretch inside the delts and %.

Upright Row

If you have got got get right of entry to to a pulley machine, use it for this workout. Otherwise a barbell will do.

Hold the barbell or pulley bar inside the middle, palms down, arms touching each distinct. Stand proper now above the pulley, if possible. Pull right away up until your hands are at shoulder diploma. Keep the bar near the frame. If you pull up with the bar far from the body, the workout specializes within the anterior delt best. Hold for a second and then decrease and repeat.

Dumbbell Curls

Begin with a dumbbell in each hand, fingers handling lower back. You can boom your balance and decrease today's strain inside the route of the workout thru performing the motion leaning in competition to a bench along aspect your knees barely bent.

Think of the exercise as a combination of movements that should be smoothly included. First, supination of the forearm. This is really rotating the forearm so your palm, which begins offevolved offevolved facing backward, finally subsequently ends up going through ahead.

Second, a curl. Proper curling shape isn't always apparent, nor is it what the frame honestly does, if given a threat. The natural tendency with any workout is to do as little artwork as viable. When doing curls, for instance, your body adjusts to the placement of quality mechanical benefit, taking as heaps stress off your biceps as feasible – in no way what you want to boom your biceps.

To maximize the artwork executed with the aid of your biceps in the course of any curl you need to make sure that your elbows continue to be in close to the frame. Moving the elbow faraway from the frame takes most of the strain off the biceps and locations possibly adverse strain on the elbows. You must moreover preserve your elbow barely in the front of you in some unspecified time in the future of the curl. The natural tendency is

to permit the elbow pass next to the body –
or worse, inside the back of the frame – as
you decorate the burden. This furthermore
takes the stress off the frame.

When performing a supinated curl, both the
supination of the forearm and the curling
movement need to occur simultaneously. The
supination need to no longer show up . Try to
rotate the forearm easily sooner or later of
the whole curling motion. Remember to
deliver your elbow inside the front of you to
make certain most movement of the long
head of the bicep, which flees the shoulder as
well as the elbow.

Lean into the curl on the top to preserve
tension at the biceps.

On the way down it is critical to exactly
opposite the motion performed on the way
up.

Flyes

Lie face up on a flat bench. Rest your ft at the
quit of the bench to save you your decrease

again from arching in the route of the exercising. Grasp a dumbbell in each hand and expand your arms proper away up, palms coping with every exclusive. Your elbows ought to now not be bent.

Lower the weights to each facet to honestly beneath the level of the bench. The weights — and your palms — must stay perpendicular on your frame thru your shoulders. Feel for the stretch for the duration of the midline of the p.C.. Your palms want to turn out to be at proper angles to your frame. To lower likely dangerous strain for your biceps and elbows, your elbows want to be slightly bent at the lowest of the motion, collectively along with your hands above bench diploma.

Moving in the most important arc feasible, bring the weights over again as heaps because the start characteristic. Keep your hands inner the precise plane. Do no longer increase the bend in the elbows. If you do, the emphasis will shift from the % to the triceps. At the peak of the motion, your shoulders should upward push up off the bench slightly as you bring the weights collectively.

Concentrate on feeling the exercising at some stage in your chest and not on your shoulders.

Calf Raises

Stand together along side your feet on the block of a status calf decorate device, your heels extending out into place. Hook your shoulders beneath the pads and straighten your legs, lifting the burden clean of the beneficial useful resource. Lower your heels as a ways as feasible towards the ground, maintaining your knees barely bent sooner or later of the motion if you want to art work the lower place of the calves in addition to the better location, and feeling the calf muscle mass stretch to the maximum. From the bottom of the movement, come up on your ft as some distance as viable. The weight need to be heavy enough to exercise the calves, but no longer so heavy that you cannot come all the manner up for maximum of your repetitions.

Side Lateral Raises

Hold dumbbells, one in each hand, at your components, palms going via your aspects. Lift the weights out to the aspect, pretending that, in place of dumbbells, you have got were given were given pitchers of water in each hand and that you're going to water some flora up at shoulder degree.

Allow your elbows to bend and your forearms to pressure barely beforehand out of the proper plane. As you acquire the pinnacle of the movement, rotate your shoulders beforehand so the front plates of the dumbbells are barely decrease than the rear plates – simply as if you had been pouring water. This will enhance your elbows barely. The rotation should pop out of your shoulders, now not your wrists or arms.

The pouring motion positions the lateral deltoid to take the brunt of the stress. If you don't pour, the Anterior Deltoid allows out too much, lowering the performance of the exercise.

Dumbbell Shoulder Press

Sitting on a bench, preserve one dumbbell in every hand at shoulder peak, elbows out to the factor, hands handling in advance. Lift the dumbbells at once up till they contact at the pinnacle, then decrease them all over again as an extended manner as viable. You will discover that you are succesful of each increase and decrease the dumbbells farther than you may a barbell, regardless of the truth that the want to control weights independently approach that you are lifting barely a great deal less poundage.

Chapter 4: Putting It All Together

You now have the blueprint for building the today's you. Follow the advice on this ebook over the next one year and you WILL percent amongst 10 and 30 solid pounds of muscle tissues onto your frame. If that doesn't sound like a bargain to you, go out and seize maintain of a pound of lean steak. Now, keep in mind a dozen or so of those cuts of high pork slapped within the course of your frame. Believe me, which will make a dramatic distinction to the way that you appearance!

As you tour alongside your journey to a more huge body, you can come across all varieties of properly which means folks that will provide you recommendation, frown at what you're doing and try to sell you at the modern-day-day certain hassle. Your project, however, is to live centered on the two exercising levels with a view to be your education life over the subsequent three hundred and sixty 5 days. Too many human beings get began on a top notch trouble and then transfer to some difficulty else in advance than giving it time to work. Don't be one of them.

Where to from proper right here?

Reclaiming your body, grasping maintain of your bodily future and forging the frame that you choice is ready more than information.

It's about motion.

This book has given you the data. In fact it has supplied a template of precisely what you want to do – and avoid – in an effort to sculpt the frame of your dreams, despite your genetic limitations. The query is . . .

What are you going to do with that expertise?

Are you going to be similar to the 70% of people who purchase exercise and vitamins publications and do . . .

Nothing?

Are you going to use the clean direction we've furnished on vitamins, and proper, clinical training OR are you going to keep spinning your wheels, flitting from one unproductive training routine to a few other with no longer something to expose for it?

Are you going to take the exercising mission, forget about the archaic nonsense approximately genetic obstacles, and use the iron to shape and remodel your body OR are you going slip lower again onto the couch and resume the pass nowhere manner of life which has formed the body that you now personal?

Are you going to transform your intellectual landscape, energizing it with the electricity of cause placing and terrific questioning to catapult you ahead like an unstoppable cyborg OR are you going to languish in a international of stinking questioning, convincing yourself which you are not capable of construct muscle, get in shape and make traction for your existence?

Chapter 5: Advantages Of Muscle Building

There are many blessings of obtaining a splendidly toned body form. These are the subsequent:

1. It makes you appearance splendid.

No count the manner you try to cover it, it's far the number one reason of most ladies and men. Those who are tired of being thin and dangerous will need a suit and attractive frame. That is why more and more ladies and men want to be in remarkable shape. Looking perfect isn't a criminal offense.

2. It promotes recurring workout.

If you are the type of character who does not want repetitive sports activities, perhaps you will be expert to like everyday sporting activities. Being on a muscle constructing software program calls as a manner to have a recurring exercise that takes few hours of your day. It is a laugh and in the end, you'll learn how to consciousness on the venture. Then getting used to the dependancy will truely arise.

three. It paves the way for a healthy way of life.

When you need to appearance high-quality, a wholesome way of life will follow. You will save you all that carbohydrate-rich food, junks, and alcoholic drinks at the same time as you purpose for a body that is to die for. It is real that when you have an exercise application, you will include your food plan as a part of your plan.

4. It boosts your vanity.

When you like the way you appearance, it'll actually show. Believe it or not, it's going to create a one-of-a-type glow for your face. It will arouse your self perception, in any other case growth a good buy notion in yourself. When you are assured in the way you appearance, you'll be able to exchange the manner you deal with issues, duties, relationships and greater.

Chapter 6: Work Out Training

To advantage the very great fine benefit from a body constructing exercising, you may need to utilize hundreds of exercises which deal with each part of your body and focus on the various groupings of muscle corporations. Using weights, weight gadget, and aerobic hobby that get the cardiovascular device pumping are all factors of a wholesome utility. If you are asking your self which types of frame building carrying sports may be maximum beneficial, there is no one-duration-suits-all blueprint for all people.

An Approach for Starters If you are just getting commenced out and were pretty inert for a great duration, you need to first take an stock of your fitness - perhaps via a private scientific practitioner - earlier than beginning. Your fitness and fitness can appreciably factor into your recoverability, susceptibility to harm, and frame obstacles.

By setting out a frame constructing exercise consultation for the number one objective of fitness, you may likely must get commenced out incrementally and paintings your manner up - in particular if it's miles been severa years since you formerly engaged. Another bodybuilding exercising trouble is your man or woman goals. What are you after - dropping weight, constructing strength, normal health, or perhaps a mixture of those? What making a decision - plus your gift fitness - will basically establish the kind of frame building exercise software software you're taking component in.

To be powerful with the resource of having primary records, you want to have a massive consciousness of human frame shape, in which splendid muscle businesses are placed throughout your frame, along element their easy characteristic. Becoming equipped with specifics just like the ones will help in your steerage, You can then offer hobby to centered muscle companies, the use of weights to enhance and form them.

Consider the Time Commitment. Do now not experience as if you have to initially devote your self every day to operating out - possibly a 4-day exercise week may be sufficient. A logical exercise schedule, as an example, need to thoroughly be executed on Monday, Wednesday, Thursday, and Friday along with your break days on Wednesday and also the weekend - some thing days agree with your way of life. Beginning a bodily workout plan this manner will, on eventually of the week best, hit each muscle business enterprise bearing in mind each most suitable muscle healing time and increase potential.

Your Muscles Require a Break We may not commonly be inclined to endure in mind resting the muscle companies as a period for recuperation, regardless of the truth that that is what's taking place when you paintings them difficult sooner or later and allow them a time off the subsequent. This healing duration is crucial for the lengthy-term improvement of muscle growth and ordinary health and health.

Maintain a document of the physical video games you carry out and have a look at your development regularly. The notably little time it requires to put in writing down down a small range of comments will possibly be paid lower back as you find out how your body has been reinforced over time - even greater so on those mornings whilst you in truth do now not revel in inspired to make the effort to exercise session. Moreover, you may then make modifications as needed to recognize your specific targets.

Chapter 7: Exercising Right

How to Figure Out the Best Type of Exercises

The extraordinary shape of sports sports for bodybuilding may also additionally variety depending upon your bodily country. They also can variety also depending upon your energy degree or persistence. Just the identical, if bodybuilding hobbies you as a hobby or a professional career then some sports may be greater useful to you than others.

Lifting weights obviously will have masses to do with frame constructing. This bodily video games is as an alternative honest at the begin. The concept is that you can increase and push heavy weights spherical and gain muscle. The muscle can then be toned and higher defined at some point of your parent with non-prevent work and workout workouts.

First it can be vital to apprehend, however, that you may best start doing this from a right weight. What a right weight is will range, however it worries your percentage of frame fats. If your body is carrying more weight within the form of fat then you may be less ready to start with an effective bodybuilding method. The extra weight will need to be dropped in order a good way to benefit muscle.

Provided you are ready to start a normal exercising normal there are a few stuff you need to maintain in thoughts. For one, there are numerous physical games to be had on the manner to do or declare to do a variety of factors for you. Provided they'll be reliable, you could nonetheless need to recognize wherein your weaknesses are. If you want a software program targeted greater upon your lower again and shoulders then you may consider that, and so on.

As to the tremendous sort of physical video video games for building muscle, if you want to trade too from individual to individual. It can also assist to keep in mind, even though, that you'll commonly be looking for a device regarding a low rep depend and immoderate weight quantity together collectively together with your bodily sports. You also can do an exercise most effective a handful of instances, however with a excessive diploma of intensity.

For example if you may usually curl handiest twenty pounds ten instances, you may need to attempt curling thirty or 40 pounds 5 instances. This device will normally bring about proper income in muscles. This gain in muscle tissue works by means of manner of growing the pressure at the muscle and in fact growing small tears. The healing tool your frame undertakes to heal the ones tears creates extra muscles.

Considering this, it is able to moreover result in massive and more fast earnings in case your workout includes a number of compound lifts instead of isolation lifts. The compound carry requires that multiple joint as having artwork completed along it. A right example is the bench press. The joints being applied with a bench press are the shoulders and elbows, in place of an isolation deliver just like the curl which first-rate includes the elbow.

These compound lifts require more than honestly one muscle organization and consequently assist you to do more with a lot much less time. That does no longer suggest you ought to neglect really about isolation lifts, as they will be used to growth your muscle mass in a particular location. This is probably crucial if you have a specific area of your frame this is lots tons much less defined or sturdy. By consisting of each isolation and compound lifts for your physical video games you've got were given if you want to beautify your bodybuilding.

With all this in mind you may with a piece of good fortune improvement quicker as you pursue a body constructing recurring. With a proper regular you could become stronger and larger as you preference, too.

The Best Type of Exercises for Body Building

The nice form of sports for bodybuilding is probably of gain for a extremely good deal greater than clearly growing strong muscle tissue. These sports activities will assist to amplify flexibility and help cardiovascular health, all on the same time as developing energy. Developing strength and fitness in this way may also actually have quality benefits for mental and ordinary physical fitness. Bodybuilding might be the healthiest hobby that a person can participate in. This is why bodybuilding is so famous, it can make you enjoy real and it can make you look top too.

The extremely good sorts of weight education physical games for muscle increase are compound lifts; those are wearing activities that rent multi-joint actions. This type is extra herbal than isolation sports activities, and promotes a extra severe workout. Working many muscle agencies in a unmarried workout will sell the release of muscle building hormones and could burn greater power. These sporting sports are also extra useful for normal capability.

There are many techniques to do weight education wearing sports activities. The most beneficial style of gadget to use to supply the wished weight is unfastened weights. Free weights first-rate simulate natural frame movements; they artwork the muscle corporations being targeted and the middle muscle mass which stabilize the body. This makes the frame an entire lot much a good deal less likely to undergo damage. Free weights moreover advise that on every repetition slight versions arise as a manner to reduce the probability of plateaus going on wherein no development takes location.

Good kinds of bodybuilding exercising sporting activities will emphasize movements which is probably prolonged. For example squats and bench presses, in vicinity of shoulder shrugs and calf presses. These exercise exercises are lot more intense as extra art work has to be achieved in every repetition. They furthermore typically generally tend to include greater muscle groups, at the side of the center muscle units.

When seeking to construct muscular tissues it is quality to do a small amount of repetitions with a excessive weight. Select a weight so that when 4 to five repetitions the muscle is simply too tired to do each different repetition. But earlier than walking at that depth do a whole lot of repetitions at 1/2 of that weight to warmness the muscle mass up and lubricate the joints. This warm up is wanted to lessen the probabilities of damage and damage.

Chapter 8: How To Get Your Muscle Building Routine Right

One of the number one assets you want to intention to set up even before you pass all out on consuming is to have a plan to your muscle constructing. This method that you need to increase a robust muscle constructing routine involves of sports, physical games, meals and dietary dietary supplements which might be suitable and geared within the route of your muscle building effort. Having a suitable constructing ordinary can help you accumulate your desires easier.

The first component you want to take care of is to ensure that you are eating a wholesome and balanced healthy eating plan. Never pass the maximum important meal for muscle increase that is your breakfast, now not simplest it take its toll in your health in the long run it additionally cripples your improvement in muscle building. Only with the useful resource of having an important and healthy diet regime you can get the overall benefit of meals in your exercising exercises regime.

Second, you may additionally want to make sure your meals consist of the crucial stuff to construct muscle agencies. Carbohydrates, proteins, electricity are all important to shaping that more potent muscle shape and for this reason make sure that your meals have a number of those requirements. You can find out the ones in meat and also nutritional supplements. Chicken, mutton, red meat, fish, soy are all super supply of proteins.

Lastly, you want to have willpower and dedication to the plan you've got got laid out for your self. Aiming to be as massive as

Stallone inside a month isn't always practical and it may moreover demoralize you, consequently ensure to staying energy and hobby while you're aiming to get bigger.

Chapter 9: A Prioritization Approach To Body Building Training

In attaining and preserving focus, it's far vital which you examine the importance of prioritizing the edges of bodybuilding education and wonderful commitments in existence, to mixture a a success training recurring. The prioritization technique is, consequently, a essential issue of bodybuilding endeavors. This technique calls for that you prioritize all the education elements along with conduct, sporting events, behaviors, rest and recovery elements of training, weight-reduction plan, muscle organizations, training frequency, motor skills, education intensity and amongst others into five blocks or elements of interest.

The first is the need, the aim, the goal. What is it that you are inquisitive about, what do you want to gather via the education software program. That which is most required and targeted for must then be prioritized. After a while in education, you may realise the want for a whole frame development, in which the body is balanced in muscular mass and electricity. In this, you have to discover ways to determine the ones frame elements which may be foundational to the training and increase of diverse frame components and muscle organizations. The arms, for instance, must be prioritized in the look for electricity because of the chest, again, and abs will no longer be trained to most useful intensities if the fingers are willing. Again, there are the ones training elements that precede others and therefore it is a must for a frame builder to initiate schooling on the ones foundation factors like diet, even in advance than he or she thinks approximately constructing on depth.

This will, in turn, require which you prioritize your training based totally truly at the attention of building at the inclined, below-developed frame additives or muscle corporations. Those which have been ignored or who've no longer been optimally stimulated inside the path of boom should then be prioritized and emphasised until they are nurtured to a balanced diploma in evaluation with others.

Again, there may be a need to recognize your body internal out if you are going to broaden it optimally. In time you ought to then be able to decide the surprisingly trainable frame additives and muscle groups. In prioritizing education schedules for every precise frame detail and muscle enterprise corporation, you could, consequently, assign those fairly informed elements a whole lot less time considering with little time they'll be pushed to the maximum useful increase fee.

Finally, the prioritization method need to moreover aspect inside the desired and the to be had property to strength and facilitate the training. Equipment, time, walking shoes and food supply are but examples of the assets that want to be available in good enough portions while a software starts offevolved. It is, consequently, suitable to plot training based totally mostly on to be had belongings.

Chapter 10: Frequency Of Training During Body Building

Establishing a schooling rhythm is a cardinal requirement of a essential body builder. How regularly must a bodybuilder exercising? For how long have to each workout be? What concerns need to a bodybuilder have in mind at the same time as figuring out the proper training rhythm? This is however a number of the most not unusual questions requested thru frame developers concerning the frequency in their schooling.

To begin with, the frequency of a frame building training software program want to be based mostly on real schooling days, now not at the times of a calendar week. Each bodybuilder have to set a single precise day steady with a training week for growing one or brilliant muscle companies. Thinking in the number one terms of the calendar weekdays like Monday, Tuesday or Wednesday,and so on. Can limit bodybuilder's ability and make it a bare routine.

The frequency of schooling need to be idea of regarding day one, then day , day 3 and so on. There isn't any requirement in any respect for education days to fall on any particular calendar weekday. This ensures that interruptions are factored in efficiently, like on the same time as a body builder falls sick, the snoozing pattern has been altered, specific duties have produced fatigue that desires rest, and so on. A bodybuilding trainee need to work independently of the same old calendar.

Another attention is that not all frame muscle organizations are advanced with comparable requirements or situations. Each has a differing ratio especially the quick twitch and the sluggish twitch muscle fibers. Each skills a very unique recuperation fee and adapts to the training stimulus. The conventional case is that huge muscle groups especially quadriceps and glutes require great rest durations. The smaller muscle agencies specifically abs, shoulders, and calves get higher rapid and further successfully.

The question then remains; do superior trainees want same intervals of relaxation after working out all body muscular systems? And the solution is absolutely no, they want to not. The appropriate technique to rent is to permit differing periods for rest measured through 24 hour days. Each restoration allowance's period want to be determined with the aid of the workout intensity and a trainee's physiological capacity.

A frame builder should additionally consciously display how he or she feels within the route of and after a exercising consultation and supplement this with a 3rd celebration's professional opinion of the general common performance. A schooling accomplice is mainly beneficial in mentioning apparent underneath or overtraining signs and symptoms that the body builder would probable overlook about. Some of these signs and signs and symptoms on occasion require immediate treatment with prolonged rest intervals else they growth to too immoderate repercussions or cause injuries in the route of exercise sporting activities.

Initiate trainees are especially liable to over-acquire their education quota due to the reality enthusiasm leads them to paintings a protracted way above their degree of experience. The enthusiasm covers up for obvious beneath qualification and turns on them to paste to education programs which their individual personal genetics can not address swiftly and step by step.

Chapter 11: Nutrition

A intense bodybuilder requires an effective bodybuilding eating regimen. This ought now not to be tough but the proper bodybuilding vitamins is pretty essential for the boom of strong muscle companies. A bodybuilding healthy eating plan will recall carbohydrates in addition to the relevance they play in bodybuilding nutrients. Carbs are in fact sugars and also starches which give electricity for the body. They are separated into agencies - the smooth and complicated carbs.

Fruits, in addition to dairy products, are that that you call "easy" carbs as they're more without issues broken down through the body. Vegetables and beans are examples of "complex" carbohydrates. They take an prolonged length for the frame to approach, and they will be discovered in As a muscle builder, you can want to lessen the sort of carbohydrates for your every day food regimen specifically earlier than sound asleep at night time. Do no longer consume carbs inside an hour of bedtime due to the reality the body will not expend the strength and through the digestion of the carbohydrates, you certainly may also come to be maintaining the ones extra electricity as fat, and that's now not suitable for a bodybuilder.

When bodybuilding is big which you consume extra frequently but in lesser quantities. It is specifically endorsed that you have six smaller food every day in choice to the traditional three big food. This assists the metabolic rate live regular and additionally keeps to burn fats thru the day. Keeping the right meal schedule might be one of the most important bodybuilding vitamins methods as it will will allow you to remove fat, construct muscle and additionally be at the right direction to carrying out your goals.

Your bodybuilding food plan is an crucial element on your application to add muscles and help to your weight education route. A excellent bodybuilding plan will address all the issues of losing weight, lessening fat, building in addition to firming muscle tissues and in certainly sculpting the entire body. Proper education and moreover body building nutrients implies which you have to in no way don't forget a weight-reduction plan as hunger. Instead, it's far about making wholesome meals options and developing healthful behavior if you want to serve you properly for the rest of your existence.

Bodybuilding nutrients can be very critical that you may need to speak to a professional dietician. A bodybuilding weight loss plan is awesome from regular weight reduction diets. The recognition of a bodybuilding weight-reduction plan may be on ingesting the food as a way to can help you growth lean muscle groups and power and in case you discover this difficult, you want to invite the help of the experts. They assist you to in engaging in your intention.

Foods That Help in Body Building

Your body requires being fueled up in your exercise. Don't do your Body Building carrying sports on an empty belly. You want to hobby for your exercise.

You want to drink protein shakes: in advance than, at some point of and after your workout routines. The frame calls for protein, and shakes are not too heavy for weight lifting. You also can mixture strawberries and blueberries for a scrumptious shake.

You need to devour often. Many Body Builders eat six small food a day, spaced each to a few hours aside. This manner, you're by no means hungry. By eating often, your frame is fueled, and your muscle tissue are growing.

Chapter 12: Bodybuilding Recipes

Breakfast

Protein Pancakes

Ingredients

half cup oat flour (whole wheat or almond)

1 egg

6 oz... Fats-unfastened yogurt

1 tsp. Baking powder

Truvia or Stevia (sweetener)

Put the flour in a huge bowl andadd the egg, in case you don't want to apply an entire egg you may positioned 2 egg whites, then upload the yogurt, 1 tsp. Of baking powder and 1 or 2 tsp. Of sweetener, in keeping with private flavor. Now mixture the elements and spray a frying pan with non-stick cooking spray. Then positioned sufficient batter inside the pan for one medium length pancake and cook for forty seconds to 1 minute steady with element.

Enjoy your meal.

Protein Waffles

Ingredients

half of cup oats

1/2 cup egg whites

1 scoop of whey protein powder

1 tsp. Stevia

1/2 of cup low-fats cottage cheese/ fats-loose yogurt

1 tsp. Baking powder

Salt

Cinnamon

Take a blender and mix all of the components. If you don't have protein powder, you canput¾ of a cup of oats as a substitute. When the materials are all combined, take a waffle maker this is already warmed up and spray it with some non-stick cooking spray.

Pour a touch bit batter in each square and allow it put together dinner dinner for a few minutes. When the waffles are absolutely cooked, you can devour them easy or with a zero energy topping.

Enjoy your meal.

Spinach Omelette

Ingredients:

1 cup egg whites

Seasoning of your choice

1 ounces.. Child spinach

Pour the egg whites right into a preheated frying pan with the seasoning of your choice and sprinkle the spinach over, then located a lid on the pinnacle of the pan and allow it prepare dinner. When the eggs are cooked just, fold the Omelette in half of of and enjoy it.

Enjoy your meal.

Egg Burrito

Ingredients

1 whole wheat tortilla

1 egg

2/4 cup egg whites

Spices of your preference

Hot sauce (non-compulsory)

2 tablespoons Salsa

Spray a preheated frying pan with non-stick cooking spray and pour the egg whites and the entire egg. In the intervening time positioned the entire wheat tortilla in the microwave for approximately 20-30 seconds. When the eggs are cooked, located them within the tortilla with spices of your desire, warm sauce and a pair of tablespoons of salsa.

Enjoy your meal.

Bodybuilding desserts

Ingredients

1 cup egg whites

1 cup chopped broccoli

1/four cup chopped onions

Spices of your desire

Hot sauce (non-compulsory)

1/4 cup fat-loose shredded cheese

Take a muffin pan and spray some non-stick cooking spray. Next, take 1 cup of chopped broccoli and divide it into 6 desserts holes. Set the chopped onions set on top of the broccoli. Now take the egg whites and pour them to fill actually about¾ of the muffin hollow. You can add spices of your choice or heat sauce.To quit, pinnacle every muffin with fats-loose shredded cheese.

Cooking time: 25 minutes

Cooking temperature: 425 ranges F

Enjoy your meal.

Eggs & Oats Scramble

Ingredients

2 cup egg whites

half of of cup rolled oats (Quaker Oats)

1 egg

Spices of your desire (non-compulsory)

Put all of the components together in a bowl and mix them.

Spray a non-stick spray on the pre-heated frying pan and add the blended components.

Fry to your preferred texture for 1-2 minutes after which upload spices. Remove from warmness.

Enjoy your meal.

Protein Sandwich

Ingredients

2 slices of whole wheat bread

1 avocado

2 boiled eggs

1 Herring Fillet

Hot sauce (non-obligatory)

1 Roma tomato

1 cup diced onions

White fowl breast (a chunk)

2 tablespoons 0f canola mayonnaise

Mix 2 tablespoons of fats-free Ranch dressing, 2 tablespoons of canola mayonnaise, and a squirt of heat sauce.

Chop and add boiled eggs, avocado, Roma potato, diced the onion and the white chook breast (12.Five Oz). Mix and spread a number of these onto the complete bread,

Enjoy your meal.

Lunch And Dinner

Bodybuilding Crispy Strips

Ingredients

1 fowl breast reduce into strips

1/four cup buttermilk

2 cups all-reason flour

1 tablespoon salt

Spices of your choice

Put the buttermilk in a bowl and dip the bird strips for 15-20 mins

Mix the flour and salt (or spices).

Sprinkle the¼ of buttermilk into the flour aggregate and stir lightly.

Heat a few vegetable oil on medium heat. Get the hen strips soaked inside the buttermilk and located then on the flour mixture to coat.

When lightly lined, area the strips in the heated oil. Cook for 2 mins on every side. When crispy and golden eliminate from the oil.

Enjoy your meal.

Lemon Marinade Chicken

Ingredients

Juice of 1 lemon

2 cloves garlic, minced

2 tablespoons olive oil

1 tablespoon black pepper

1 fowl breast, skinless and boneless

Salt

Mix olive oil with garlic, lemon juice, and pepper in a baking dish with a fork. Marinate the hen breast inside the aggregate for 25 minutes. Heat the iron grill pan specifically warmth and cook dinner each side of the bird breast, on the same time as sprinkling salt, for 4-6 minutes.

Enjoy your meal.

Chicken Burgers

Ingredients

half of pound floor chook bird

2 tablespoons grated candy onion

2 tablespoons vegetable oil

1/4 tablespoons cayenne pepper

2 cups coarse clean bread crumbs

1 tablespoons coarse-grained salt

1/2 of of cup low-fats milk

Mix 1 cup breadcrumbs, pepper, onion, cayenne, and milk in a blending ambitious and place the fowl there. Divide the beef into 2 and shape them into patties. Use the remaining 1 cup bread crumbs to coat the patties.

Heat the vegetable oil on medium heat and fry the patties for 5 mins every side.

Enjoy your meal.

Turkey Burger

Ingredients

half of of pound floor turkey meat

2 tablespoons grated sweet onion

2 tablespoons vegetable oil

1/4 tablespoon cayenne pepper

2 cups coarse glowing bread crumbs

1 tablespoon coarse-grained salt

half of of of cup low-fat milk

Mix 1 cup breadcrumbs, pepper, onion, cayenne, and milk in a mixing formidable and place the turkey meat there. Divide the beef into 2 and shape them into patties. Use the final 1 cup bread crumbs to coat the patties.

Heat the vegetable oil over medium warmth and fry the patties for five minutes each aspect.

Enjoy your meal.

Chicken Parmesan

Ingredients

Tomato sauce

2 thin chook cutlets

Salt

Cooking spray

2 egg whites

three tablespoons cooking oil

2 tablespoons grated Parmesan

1 cup shredded cheese

6 tablespoons dry bread crumbs

Heat the oven to 420 tiers F. Spray the cooking spray on a baking dish. Sprinkle the fowl with salt and beat the egg in a bowl. Mix the Parmesan and the bread crumbs on a sheet of paper. Put the flour on a fantastic paper. Dip the chicken into flour after which dip into the egg whites. Coat the chook with the crumbs.

Heat the cooking oil on medium warm temperature. Add the fowl and prepare dinner for 5 mins. When organized location it in a unique bowl. Add sauce to the fowl and then smear the hen with the cheese. Bake for 10-15 mins until the cheese soften.

Enjoy your meal.

Oven-Fried Chicken

Ingredients

three chicken breast, cut into strips

¼ cup butter or margarine

½ cup all-motive flour

1 teaspoon paprika

½ teaspoon salt

¼ teaspoon pepper

Preheat oven to 425 levels F. Melt the butter in the oven then receives rid of it. Mix flour with paprika, pepper, and salt then use the aggregate to coat the hen. Put the fowl inside the pan and bake each element for 20 mins.

Enjoy your meal.

Cauliflower Rice

Ingredients

1 big head cauliflower

2 tablespoon cooking oil (non-compulsory)

Remove any leaves and then wash the cauliflower

Grate cauliflower to the dimensions of rice with a subject grater the region on a easy towel to absorb extra moisture.

Put cooking oil in a frying pan over medium warm temperature for 1 minute then add the cauliflower. Cover with a lid and prepare dinner for 7-10 mins.

Enjoy your meal.

Lasagna

Ingredients

4 lasagna noodles, cooked and worn-out

2 eggs

2 cup ricotta cheese

2 cups shredded mozzarella cheese

1 pound floor red meat

1/2cup grated Parmesan cheese

1 jar (forty five oz.) Sauce

Mix mozzarella cheese, 1 cup Parmesan cheese, eggs, and ricotta cheese in a bowl and region it apart.

Cook the beef over medium-immoderate warmth in a saucepan after which stir inside the sauce.

Preheat oven to 375 ranges F

In baking dishes, spoon 1 cup meat in each and upload 2 lasagna noodles to every. Add the cheese mixture and Parmesan cheese.

Bake for half of of-hour and go away to chill for 15 minutes.

Enjoy your meal.

Desserts

Blueberry Muffins

Ingredients

1/2 cup margarine

2 cups all-purpose flour

21/2 cups glowing blueberries

2 big eggs

1 cup granulated sugar

1/2 cup milk

1 teaspoon vanilla

2 teaspoons baking powder

1/four teaspoon salt

Non-stick cooking spray

Mix the granulated sugar with margarine using the electric mixer. While stirring, add one egg at a time. Beat in vanilla located thru baking powder and salt.

Add half of flour after which half milk on the identical time as stirring and repeat it.

Fold within the blueberries gently.

Spoon int0 the muffin cup and onto every muffin sprinkle topping

Bake for 10-20 minutes

Enjoy your meal.

Peanut Butter Cookies

Ingredients

1 cup butter

2 cups all-purpose flour

1 cup peanut butter

2 eggs

1 cup white sugar

1 teaspoons baking soda

1 cup brown sugar

1 teaspoon baking powder

1/2 teaspoon salt

Mix the sugars, butter, and peanut butter. Sift the flour, baking soda, baking powder and salt then stir it into the combination. Refrigerate the dough for 1 hour.

Heat the oven to 375 stages F

Shape the dough into balls (about 1 inch). With a fork flatten the balls in a crisscross sample.

 Bake for 9-10 mins till they may be brown.

Enjoy your meal.

Banana Muffins

Ingredients

2 massive bananas, mashed

1 egg 1/3 cup butter, melted

1 1/2 cups all-reason flour

1 teaspoon baking powder

3/four cup white sugar

1 teaspoon baking soda

1/2 of teaspoon salt

Heat oven to 350 tiers F. Sift the flour, baking soda, salt, and baking powder collectively. Coat muffin pans with non-stick spray.

Mix sugar, banana, melted butter and egg in big bowl and then upload the flour mixture at the identical time as stirring.

Spoon into muffin pans and bake for 20-25 mins.

Enjoy your meal.

French Toast

Ingredients

1 teaspoon Vanilla Extract

4 slices bread

1 egg

half of teaspoon Cinnamon, Ground

1/four cup milk

Beat the egg in a shallow bowl, then blend with cinnamon and vanilla. Stir the aggregate in milk.

Dip the bread inside the aggregate then fry the slices until they'll be golden brown.

Enjoy your meal.

Pancakes

Ingredients

2 cups all-cause flour

1½ cups milk

2 teaspoon baking powder

2 tablespoon butter, melted

2 tablespoon vegetable oil

½ teaspoon salt

Chapter 13: Dietary Supplements

The system of frame building can be prolonged and a tough one. The dietary nutritional supplements are required for helping the body and making the frame reply quicker. The nutritional supplements are super in the occasion that they include nutritional merchandise in desire to artificial content material. There are a number of in genuine products inside the marketplace that have names much like famous ones. The supplements will paintings first-class if they're of remarkable fine and consist of the right form of components.

There are the various dietary supplements with precise nutritional fee, and some of them are made from completely natural products and due to this are very secure. Still, it's miles continuously more regular to take underneath the steering of the expert and function entire know-how in advance than choosing up one.

Importance of Bodybuilding Supplements

When building more potent muscular tissues the method that is going on is that the muscle tissues are labored to the point of harm, then they get better through rebuilding in a stronger shape. This technique that time desires to be left among exercise periods to allow this recuperation and rebuilding device. For a novice exercising instructions can take place every different day. But because of the fact the muscle corporations get more potent the strain placed on them is a terrific deal extra and healing time is longer. This manner that the c programming language amongst classes wishes to be longer.

The higher forms of wearing sports will consist of a few cardio art work. The most important kind of cardio is c language schooling, and a brilliant manner of doing that may be a exercise. Sports that incorporate lots of surprising burst of immoderate artwork are the fantastic kinds, such things as basketball are exquisite. This sort of aerobic is higher for the joints and provides a awesome exercising for the heart. Therefore, so it's miles an lousy lot less difficult to stay with.

The first-rate type of physical video video games for bodybuilding goals the help of a amazing eating regimen. A healthy food plan will permit the frame to assemble muscle correctly. A right diet plan may additionally additionally promote fitness and make it a whole lot less complicated to do all the important exercise.

Types of Supplements Available in The Market

There are nice health worries concerning the results of body building nutritional dietary supplements. Some people have this contemporary notion of bodybuilding dietary supplements as terrible to at the least one's fitness. While there is uncertainty about the effectiveness of such merchandise, we're able to bargain the reality that there may be genuinely FDA-permitted (Food and Drug Administration) body constructing dietary dietary supplements, which proves to be effective and healthful to use. It is all about following the instructions and dosage carefully and selecting the dependable and dependable manufacturers within the marketplace these days.

There are many manufacturers of bodybuilding dietary nutritional supplements within the market in recent times. To recognize more about them, test out the statistics underneath on body building nutritional dietary dietary supplements.

Protein Powders

From the choice itself, it's miles to be had in powder shape to be mixed with water, juice or sprinkled on meals. A shaker bottle could probably be available for smooth blending of protein powders specifically even as you are constantly at the pass and want your protein repair in advance than or after your exercise. Protein powders are used as pre-training consultation dietary supplements to beautify strength and assist in muscle constructing. While protein is available in the food that we devour, folks who training consultation masses and do muscle or weight training need that greater quantity of protein this is critical for muscle formation. Other protein powders moreover work as placed up-workout a complement to restore muscle groups that wear out for the duration of schooling session. You can browse positioned up workout dietary supplements online to understand extra of what those can do for you.

Energy Boosters

Working out on a normal basis can leave us exhausted and fatigued. Work out on a everyday foundation and though work 8-9 hour shifts, feels a deadbeat. We might be tumbling to mattress as fast as we get home and could likely sense exhausted even as we wake up. Caffeine can boom our power and prevent sleepiness. However, there are power-boosting nutritional nutritional supplements that humans can now motel to when they need to enjoy invigorated every day. This will assist you sense energized even after a strenuous workout. Energy boosters can also help reduce fatigue and boom our strength to exercise session even extra. This is right for folks who juggle an entire lot of obligations like paintings and family.

Weight Loss Supplements

Alongside the body constructing functionality of sure supplements, there are also products geared inside the direction of weight loss to supply greater powerful results. While giving the body its protein and vital vitamins to enhance muscle building, weight reduction supplements also are designed to burn fat successfully. These will assist you reduce weight and advantage muscle agencies at a quicker fee. Compared to weight reduction tablets, this frame constructing supplement is nice effective on the equal time as complemented with ordinary exercise session. Otherwise, a sure fitness danger can also additionally moreover arise.

Chapter 14: Understanding Mass Muscle Building

If you are constantly within the health club running with weights, you then virtually probable are not handiest one in search of to lose fat however moreover advantage muscle mass. Although there are extraordinary muscles, just like the cardiac muscle or your heart, we are capable of focus on skeletal muscle tissues, as they seem to be the problem right right here. Skeletal muscle mass are composed of thread-like myofibrils and sarcomeres that form a muscle fiber which can be the important gadgets of contraction.

These skeletal muscle groups in a human frame settlement after they acquire signs from motor neurons, which is probably introduced on by manner of sarcoplasmic reticulum. The better you're at controlling your muscle corporations or sending them to agreement, the stronger you could turn out to be.

So at the same time as a powerlifter is able to growth heavy weights despite the fact that he doesn't seem like so cumbersome, it's because of his functionality to spark off his motor neurons and agreement his muscle businesses better. Some powerlifters may be small in comparison to 3 bodybuilders, however they're able to considerably bring extra weights.

THE PHYSIOLOGY OF MUSCLES GROWTH

After a exercising, your body automatically replaces broken muscle fibers. It fuses muscle fibers collectively to form new myofibrils Or muscle protein strands. These repaired myofibrils are advanced to create muscle mass growth. Muscle growth occurs while the rate of muscle protein synthesis is extra than the price of protein breakdown. This, but, occurs no longer on the time of your actual exercise but while you are at rest.

3 MECHANISMS THAT MAKE MUSCLES GROW

Behind the development of the herbal muscle boom is its capacity to region greater pressure on the muscles, which can be a first-rate aspect involved within the boom of a muscle, and disrupts homeostasis inside your body. These stresses and common disruptions in homeostasis motive three important mechanisms to cause muscle growth.

Tension

To stimulate your muscle businesses to broaden, you need to apply extra stress for your body extra than it normally has. The primary way to do that is thru lifting heavy weights. This extra anxiety to your muscle groups causes the change within the chemistry of your muscle organizations, permitting muscle companies boom and satellite tv for pc cellular activation. Muscular anxiety additionally influences the relationship of the motor devices and muscle cells.

Muscle Damage

After a exercise and you enjoy an harm in your muscular tissues, this local muscle harm causes the release of inflammatory molecules and immune tool cells, which spark off satellite tv for pc television for computer cells and waft them into movement. This does no longer typically imply however that you feel soreness for your muscle companies.

Metabolic Stress

After a exercising and you feel the burnout after the exercise, then you definitely surely experience the reaction to metabolic strain. Bodybuilders may say that the "pump" motives their muscle agencies to become large. Metabolic strain causes swelling of cells throughout the muscle, which contributes to the muscle agencies increase without genuinely increasing the scale of the muscle cells. This is largely because of the addition of muscle glycogen, which motives the muscle companies to swell collectively with connective tissue boom. This increase is what we call sarcoplasmic hypertrophy.

Chapter 15: The Renegade Method

Not all men are reduce for most of that inflexible body constructing schooling habitual available. If you're each thin or fat suffering to advantage strength, lose fat, and boom muscle groups however genetically common, then you definately definately in fact should no longer deal with frame constructing program or education as a way to never paintings for average guys.

Most of these will assist you to understand to...

Always skip heavy

Always do complete body workout exercises

Do crunches and cardio to amplify you a six %

Do now not some thing else however the Olympic lifts and huge electricity

Have 6-7 meals in an afternoon

Eat 2 grams of protein in line with pound of body weight.

Avoid carbohydrates and isolation wearing sports

Spend a super deal on supplements

If you don't need to amplify harm and waste time and money challenge the ones training applications that received't provide you with the results you want, then higher keep away from them. You need a better software program application than the ones – a software program specially designed for skinny or fats, damage-willing hard gainers and advocated even for those over 35 years of age.

Background

John Davies primarily based the Renegade schooling, a throwback to a time whilst there's no alternative apart from victory itself. Davies preaches a hardcore warrior approach in getting geared up trainees for the battles competing for lifestyles and victory. This particular technique has advanced dominant athletic forces with an super regularity. His trainees range from NFL and football elite to weekend warriors who all share a outstanding obsession for victory.

Sad to say, schooling in recent times has departed from its real characteristic and reason, it really is to improve simple overall performance whether or not in the region of opposition or life. As you need to gain your fitness, fitness, and common usual overall performance dreams, you need to set apart the photos and exercising standards and virtually encompass the idea that every one bodily sports want to create a high-quality form, efficient motion, and impenetrable to accidents.

THE METHOD

The Renegade is particularly designed for the common thin and fat tough gainers who dreamed of getting a genuinely best frame weight and a super frame constructed but . . .

Don't have masses time to spend on prolonged hours of schooling

Not lucky to inherit extraordinary genetics for building muscle and energy

Are now not on steroids and different overall performance-enhancement tablets

Are able to increase sufficient injuries from workout physical activities in location of developing muscular tissues.

Concepts of Training

Movements skilled, no longer musculature

Motor patterning and grafting

Stabilization inside the maximum destabilized education environments

Postural alignment is perfected

Force advanced such this is may be projected, time-commemorated and redirected at maximal ranges.

Analyzing the ones ideas, concrete structures are pretty obvious and honest to the reason of accomplishing a better ordinary performance. While maximum education is centered in a unmarried area, usually more weight room sports activities, little or on occasion no factor out of other attributes needed to maximize commonplace overall performance. To in truth excel, an athlete should personal more a ways-accomplishing attributes, every of which identical power and functionality.

Determination and Dedication

Drive

Range of Motion – dynamic and static

Linear Speed

Agility

Strength – numerous office work

Sports Specific Skills

Work Threshold

Therefore, it is quite obvious that the Renegade Method of training is embracing an normal athletic development and excellence on the identical time as adopting a conglomeration of explosive power and enchantment. Clearly, the critical issue to this delicate mixture is the idea of education whilst perfecting the seamless and green movements.

Under the Renegade software program, you can anticipate a advantage of eighty 4 pounds of muscle businesses in a month in case you are simply going to in truth check every coaching. However, you want to position inside the required effort and time.

The purpose why maximum people in no manner benefit the popular stop result is because they typically normally have a tendency to make shortcuts and search for an a lot much less difficult and accessible manner for them. Discipline, willpower, and staying electricity are all part of the education. This is not all about bodily results but patience in all thing is a want to toward the victory you want to gain or a few element purpose you have were given set for your self.

The Rules

#1 – Build Muscles for Strength

Don't count on to convert your frame constructed via doing the equal exercise over and over. You have compelled a alternate to arise and the right way to try this is through along side weights to the bar. Get more potent thru the usage of starting inside the type of 5-10 reps and you'll get bigger. Heavy schooling gives top notch consequences than slight training.

While doing this, it's far crucial to set up your very personal non-public records. Pick up a few physical activities and list down those you could begin to do with 6-eight reps. Work over your way over the subsequent few weeks or months until you could be capable of add spherical 10-20 pounds to each of these lifts or do 3-five reps with the identical weight. Doing this innovative hobby will strain your body to develop.

As speedy as you achieve the higher give up of the rep variety upload weight and begin over with 6. This is easy however effective and the bottom line proper right here is to get huge to get robust.

#2 – Utilize Compound Muscle-Building Exercises

The form of workout in that you applied the first-rate quantity of weight and which lets in you the first-rate percentage of will boom in loading are the ones to help you build muscular tissues speedy! Remember, you aren't going to expand with a exercise the use of elliptical machines, and so on. You need to load your frame with inflexible carrying sports so one can persuade your frame which you want greater muscular tissues and energy.

Here are a number of the nice compound weights schooling sports activities for constructing muscle tissues.

Military Presses – dumbbell. Barbell, kettlebell, and log

Squats - -Front, back, buffalo bar, safety bar, and belt.

Low Incline Presses – Dumbbells and barbells

Rows – one-arm dumbbells, chest supported landmine

Sled Work – dragging and pushing

Loaded Carries – go through hug, racked, shouldered, farmers, and zerchers

You can get strong on those sporting occasions whilst slowly which include weights and reps. You try and flow into massive numbers on those lifts for gadgets of 6-10 reps and also you're positive to get large!

#3: Complement Big Lifts with Bodyweight Exercises

Huge compound dumbbells and barbell lifts are extremely good but for a well-rounded frame built and harm-free training, you want greater than that. You should supplement those sports with an equal quantity of muscle building bodyweight sporting activities consisting of:

Chin ups

Single leg squats and lunge variations

Dips

Inverted rows

Glute ham growth

Pushup versions

Plank versions for middle power/stability and to guard your decrease lower lower again

#four: Use Perfect Technique for Building Muscle Safely

Use the following steering to collect a clearly best method for bodybuilding.

Get your whole body tight from head to foot. As you squeeze at the bar or dumbbell, squeeze it which includes you're approximately to crush it. If you are reputation, squeeze your "glutes" and brace your "abs".

Be positive to govern the reducing of the bring in 2-3 seconds.

Stretch your muscle inside the bottom characteristic however don't move too deep, because it will reason damage. You should no longer enjoy any stress for your joints.

Reverse the movement and begin the effective portion of the raise by using contracting your reason muscle tissues forcefully.

Never use excessive momentum.

When on massive sports activities activities, you need to fasten out on the pinnacle and reset. On dumbbells and body weight, you want to save you and just shy of a lockout on the top then proper away reverse the motion.

To build muscle businesses, usually reflect onconsideration on steady anxiety and non-stop movement. Never bypass proper proper right into a fitness center and simply begin lifting the burden. This is a positive way to increase harm and severely compromise meant outcomes.

#5: Train with the Optimal Amount of Volume

The terrific muscle constructing rep range for thin men and beginners is five-eight. After about a couple of years of non-stop training, you may boom your rep and begin on a few gadgets of 10-12 reps further to the decrease rep activities. As you get more superior in training and in age, e.G. Forty years vintage or extra, you can need to spend more time within the 8-12 reps range and lots an awful lot less within the five-7 degrees. This will shield your joints and reduce damage hazard.

While the range of reps consistent with set is important on your schooling, the same need to artwork with the whole variety of reps you do consistent with muscle organization. Research has disclosed that about 30-60 popular reps in line with muscle group are had to maximize boom. This best way that when you have a median of 6 consistent with reps set, then you definately simply need to do as a minimum 5 normal gadgets and higher to 10 for that specific muscle company. Therefore, it is advocated to begin on the low quit of the dimensions and handiest boom the quantity in case you need to.

While you get more superior for your schooling, you can artwork in degrees of each higher and reduce quantity via a right and everyday training utility.

It is in opposition to the regular hard gainer's rule to feature some better rep gadgets and greater amount. It is meant to be a few gadgets of low reps on bench presses, deadlifts, and squats. Guys doing it the possibility manner spherical come to be getting more fats and injured and they don't develop plenty muscle as they will.

After a few heavy works, do a little gadgets of slightly better reps and get a pump. Try to attention at the muscle you are trying to build and squeeze difficult every effort out of it for 8-12 rounds. After three years of right education, you will find out that danced-enhancing techniques like relaxation-pause gadgets can be very effective while used sparingly. Just don't overdo the usage of them.

#6: Muscle-Building Workout Split

The first thing you need to recognize right right here is that 3-four tough days of training each week is nice for most steroid-free and average human beings.

The 2d aspect you want to recognize is the reality that the extra not unusual you can educate a muscle organization; the better is your gain to some extent. Then the following element you need to address is the training frequency for every muscle organization. You should train with the frequency that:

Allows you to advantage the finest energy earnings

Does not create accidents on your joints and spines

Allows you to get better nicely

As your education age will boom, the frequency at which you may teach each muscle group commonly decreases no matter the fact that high-frequency training is a favourite within the fitness enterprise and no matter the reality that a have a look at positioned out that the anabolic reaction to exercise handiest lasts 1-2 days.

There are research and there are real stories, however as we based totally on results of years of training, here is a encouraged muscle-building exercising.

For Beginners:

If you are simply starting out, you have to educate with 3 complete body physical activities. Do a compounded pulling and pushing movements for the better body like a press collectively along with your chin up. Then comply with it up with a compound lower body movement like a squat or a trap bar deadlift. You may additionally upload 1-2 sporting sports like loaded consists of or swing to finish it up.

For Intermediate:

Once you have got were given been knowledgeable for longer than 6 months, you may split your workout exercises into 2 one-of-a-kind days. The traditional exercising is to teach your pinnacle body in at some point and the lower body on some other day. So if you are schooling four days in in step with week, it is able to be very and easy to do.

If you're education three days in each week, you could make a rotation in your time table. Here is an example of what I am trying to relate to you right here.

Week 1

Monday and Friday - Upper frame

Wednesday – Lower Body

Friday – Upper Body

Week 2

Monday and Friday - Lower frame

Wednesday - Upper body

Friday- Lower frame

If you are education for 3 days in according to week and pick out to have set training days every week instead of the rotation scheduling, right here is some concept for that.

Concentrate on a heavy top frame on Monday, for your legs on Wednesday, and on Friday a lighter top body reps in that you bump up the reps barely with wearing sports aren't too worrying. Instead of the barbell incline press for gadgets of five-6 reps, strive doing a dumbbell or weighted pushups for devices of 8-12 reps.

For Advanced:

Most powerlifters live with an higher/lower break up as it is simple to remaining all of the time with it. But in case you are older or have a few recovery issues, better to select a push/pull or legs break up that has you education the whole lot right away as speedy as in every week.

This way, on Monday, perform a chunk carrying activities for the shoulders, chest, and triceps. On Wednesday, pay attention your sporting sports for your lower once more and biceps and for Friday, carry out a hint leg physical video video games. You also can do an arm workout on Saturday and enlarge it to a 4-day consistent with week application. Have the whole thing planned properly and it's miles positive to work well.

A normal bodybuilding software application includes too many devices and reps and makes use of the wrong bodily activities. If you lower the complete quantity and skip heavier whilst the usage of compound moves, there can be nothing wrong with a body-components break up to move wrong. In fact, it's far much less stressful to the joints. Training a muscle organization once every five-7 days is genuinely extra stable and further effective for superior lifters. However, if you need to function greater frequency, you can add a lighter set or of work for muscle organization on days apart from the muscle companies number one schooling day.

Rule #7: "Stimulate, Don't Annihilate"

Lee Haney, referred to as 8-ime Mr. Olympia popularized this quote and it method that you need to educate tough but smart.

Don't kill yourself looking to get large and robust. You had to paintings difficult however now not to the thing of taking your breath away. Remember that you want to live first and essential. Recovery is wanted after each doing all your sports and the best manner to get better is greater meals and greater rest to your body. This manner you could't educate as frequently at immoderate potential, so don't overdo it inside the fitness center questioning you may construct muscle organizations quite as speedy.

#8: Keep Conditioning Up

There are hundreds of tough gaining myths going to be had telling humans that conditioning will make you willing and small.

On the alternative, skipping conditioning will make you lazy, out of shape, and a actual fat ass. Conditioning will can help you stay lean and beautify your recovery in amongst strengths education lessons. It is beneficial to you and has to be a part of your weekly everyday.

High-Intensity Interval Training (HIIT) is established to be very effective in boosting and burning conditioning ranges at the equal time as preserving mass muscular tissues. You have to do at the least one 15-30 minute HIIT exercise each week if you are in amass building phase and a couple of-3 HIIT workout routines steady with week if you are decreasing.

In doing all your HIIT, pass as speedy and as hard as you could, probable approximately ninety-90 five percent of most attempt for 30-60 minutes. Then take a damage and coast/cruise for 60-100 twenty seconds. Repeat the gathering for an entire of 15-30 minutes.

Some alternatives might be:

Sprinting up hills

Kettlebell swings

Rowing

Swimming

Jumping rope

Sprinting at the same time as pushing or dragging a weighted sled

Sprinting on a bike with the resistance cranked up

Adding as lots because the HIIT consultation can be a 30-60 minute stroll as many days in consistent with week as you may do. You can use your telephone tracker and get as a minimum 10,000 steps every day.

#9: Make Recovery a Huge Priority

Training is a stimulus for boom but it does continually recommend your real increase. You growth in fact takes region outdoor the gymnasium at the identical time as you have become higher and now not within the path of workout workouts. Hence, in case you fail to get better, you then cannot grow.

Therefore, to make certain which you have become higher, you must adhere to the following:

Don't overdo subjects in the gym

Never train for added than an hour

Do now not use excessive tiers of psyche on each set

Have super sleep (8-9 hours in an afternoon)

Do a few meditation

Have as a minimum 15-20 minutes of mobility and self-myofascial work in step with day

Have evaluation baths and showers

Do some low-depth conditioning and/or restorative artwork in a few unspecified time within the destiny of off days

Getting a regular rubdown

#10: Eat for Health and Longevity

Junk meals are in no manner recommended even for a skinny man or woman. This form of food is risky and could without a doubt make you fats. Remember that some thing this is risky will in no manner extend at an greatest rate. So the more healthy you're, the quicker you could gain development in your schooling purpose.

If you are the skinny kind, you need to fuel your body with immoderate remarkable and nutritive food. If you feed your body with junks, you can perform like a real junk. Even your recovery can be sluggish and filled up with contamination. If you want a actual diet that will help you optimize muscle building, then your meals want to encompass the subsequent:

Lean meat (specially meat of grass-fed animals – Paleo food regimen)

Organic eggs

Naturally-caught fishes (not cultures)

Nuts, fruits, and veggies

Starches like white rice, quinoa, and root plant life (e.G. Potatoes, yam, sweet potatoes, and so on.)

Water

You can begin with 16 instances your body weight for standard strength. If you weight 160 5 pounds, then you can eat as a whole lot as 2640 strength in an afternoon. If after one week, your week isn't adding as plenty as 17 times your body weight, drop down your calorie intake to fifteen times your body weight. Allow weeks for development evaluation.

Eat about one gram of protein in step with pound of body weight in keeping with day or a hint masses a good deal less of this.

Consume 1 ½ - 3 grams of carbohydrates regular with pound of body weight relying to your body fats degree and insulin's sensitivity and activity.

Take zero.Four – 0.Forty 5 grams of fats in line with pound of bodyweight regular with day. Fat is needed for optimizing hormones, mind function, and healthful joints, but make sure not to get overboard. It is not beneficial to take more than 30 percent of your usual energy from fat.

Your breakfast need to embody protein meals, greens, and some stop result. You can also eat egg, yogurt, or smoothies. Lunch may be the same protein and inexperienced food – fish, bird, steak, salad, and so on. At time for supper, you may have protein and all carbohydrates you can manage.

During schooling days, consume a in addition serving of protein and starchy carbohydrates one hour or 1-½ hours in advance than the training. After the education, devour over again with some more of that protein and carbohydrate meal.

The number one motive in muscle constructing is to get lean, so you ought to be as low as 12% frame fats earlier than you regulate your weight loss program as tons as reputation on mass advantage. If you are fats and although devour in amount, you're incredible to benefit extra fats. Therefore, remove the extra fats first to the factor in which your abs will appear before you may start to worry about getting large.

Bonus Rule: Be Consistent

All the data furnished above might all be vain if you are not everyday with its software program. This isn't first-rate suitable for each week or months. You want to be consistent all within the route of.

Chapter 16: Pitfalls In Muscle Building

Sometimes, humans can with out issue get annoyed in terms of constructing muscular tissues. Although you might be consuming the right meals, doing the proper exercising, and improving properly amongst classes, it's miles notably tough to assemble the type of frame which you need. The look for the right constructed frequently leads guys or perhaps ladies seeking out shortcuts. Developing mass muscle is a gradual approach and consistency is rewarded with excellent consequences. But for those who are determined and motel to short fixes, most customarily, they got frustrated with their loss of development.

For great effects and to hold you at the right music, here are a few 5 commonplace pitfalls which most people regularly resort to in their look for constructing up a brief bulk and that you want to avoid in case you don't want to get annoyed with them.

Overload with Training

Thinking that lifting allow you to construct muscle groups - with greater lifts, more muscles, you then definately definately are in reality on the wrong aspect of the lane. Lifting weights for a selected duration is useful and while overdoing it will become counterproductive.

After an hour of excessive lifting, your body automatically release pressure hormones like cortisol as a way to opposite the producing of muscle tissue. So in case you are spending hours a day within the gymnasium lifting weights, better simplify your software program and reduce out useless exercising.

Forty-5 minutes of real lifting may be a wonderful workout for optimum guys and this may equate to round 6-nine fantastic bodily video games for your everyday. So in preference to spending every second trying another model of bicep curls just draw close the fundamentals and load them up. The relaxation of it gradual must be spent for a proper warmth up and actual cool-down to complete up your normal.

Deficiency in Calories

Nutrition is an essential problem for men looking for to percentage on some length. There is continuously the tremendous or the quantity to recall. For some, the concern of inclusive of fat while constructing ass muscular tissues is what usually prevented them from eating sufficient strength to look the popular earnings.

Eating enough strength produces effective consequences and whilst someone eats sufficient, it reasons the size to move up. Quality is therefore preferred over notable. And as a long way as food tremendous is involved, avoid consuming cookies and cakes. Instead, take great assets of protein, give up result, greens, and carbohydrates.

The Harder – the Better Mentality

HIT (immoderate-depth schooling) introduce the idea that the harder is higher in packing desired frame physical activities. Thus, everything is completed in circuit-style schooling, which leaves most of the lifters in fact exhausted after their bodily games. For widespread health and weight loss, this method is beneficial. On the opposite, whilst you are walking for muscle earnings, this is counterproductive and might even bring about losing some muscular tissues.

Most education is now designed for weight reduction, but in case you are a tough gainer who reveals it difficult packing on lean meat, undergo in thoughts heavy resistance and nice meals instead. Better spend some time in the gymnasium lifting weights than run thru a tortuous circuit.

Taking Shortcuts

Most those who yearn for gaining a big frame and superb muscle groups need to look a short end result. They need to hit it rapid simply so they spend more than 6 instantly days within the fitness center. This self-discipline is laudable however then again, this is counterproductive for difficult gainers.

The exceptional mistake one have to have is to lose staying power at the same time as schooling and getting annoyed with their development. Bodybuilding and getting hulked is a slow and a tough system – which makes it exquisite inside the health employer. Do no longer assume to add length too rapid but display your sports activities activities and results from each exercising. A small quantity of development is enough to keep you going. A 5-pound growth on a bench press appears too small however in case you add five pounds every workout, you can short see the exquisite outcomes. Focus on being regular in area of looking for shortcuts.

Poor Recovery plan

Lifting is in truth, a catabolic hobby. This manner it breaks down muscle fibers rather than constructing them up. Lifting serves as a stimulus to assemble greater muscular tissues at a few stage within the restoration bouts in among instructions. Therefore, what you do at the same time as you're no longer doing some exercises have pretty greater impact that while you are inside the fitness center. Even when you have the pleasant exercising plan, lack of sleep and incorrect nutrients can even though sabotage the whole lot which you have worked hard for.

Chapter 17: The Ultimate Muscle Building Diet

right proper right here are masses of encouraged diets available on a way to eat for max fitness and bodily preferred performance that we are becoming more careworn on which one is terrific for us. Some say the carb is evil whilst others say you need the carb to advantage muscle agencies. Whatever others say, right here are some critical recommendations as a manner to simply offer you with tons of strength and lifetime fitness.

Through this listing, we're aiming for the following:

Quick and clean way to lose fats

Gain lean muscle with lots less brought body fat

More power at some point of the day

Mental clarity and greater popularity

Optimized immune tool functioning

Better moods and higher sex electricity

Good digestion

Less aches, ache and reduce infection threat

 Consume Whole Foods

A nutritive diet plan aimed to accumulate mass muscular tissues and boom normal overall overall performance needs to be healthful. If your motive is sincerely everyday with this, then your weight-reduction plan need to recognition on optimizing your properly – being and extraordinary of lifestyles. If you have been no longer in a strong health and power, may want to you care to have a top notch set of abs? This can't very last forever.

While you want to understand what an most suitable diet want to embody, right here is one concept that nearly all people may additionally need to agree. A healthful food plan includes a huge type of whole food or those who aren't processed.

Potatoes, squashes, and other root flowers or tubers

Grains - rice and oats

Vegetables - of numerous sun shades, specifically the green leafy ones

Fruits - all kinds

These food are filled with important vitamins, minerals, and antioxidants plus the desired carbohydrates to fuel your training and power all through the day.

Animal Products like meat and eggs as a way to offer you:

Protein

This is essential nutrient desired in building muscle and enhancing your average universal performance. Consume one gram in keeping with pound of body weight steady with day. Don't over consume.

Healthy fat

Healthy fats are critical to lessen the risk for coronary coronary heart illness, diabetes, and continual contamination. They furthermore keep your hormones in balance.

Essential Vitamins and Minerals

There are some vital topics wished through your body that may't be furnished by way of manner of plant life. Animal meals are the effective deliver of those vitamins and minerals which includes B vitamins, copper, zinc, and iron. The combination of unprocessed vegetation and animal can provide you with the maximum vitamins content material cloth wished in gaining power and muscle constructing.

Eat Enough to Feel Energized

A wholesome food plan want to be some element that could make you feel actual and may make you preserve on with it for the relaxation of your existence. Most diets we've round us which might be supplied in books and at the Internet require you to lessen for your carbs leaving you with zero strength for exercise physical activities and your mind hazy which you run out of consciousness. How can you enlarge muscle agencies and electricity, not to say your recuperation hours if you have lots less and lots less of calories and energy-giving components.

You can't survive with a number of energy nor are you able to get on for added than 60 days.

You is probably capable of do with fewer carbs and live together with your plan however after multiple months, you'll again to the antique addiction and gain your weight decrease returned. The simplest diet you could stick on is one that may give you sufficient amount of energy to maintain recognition and be endorsed to move on.

How Much Food you want to Consume

In installing region your food plan, you want a realistic start line and proper here are some to your calorie guidelines.

For Fat Loss: 12 energy constant with pound of body weight

For Maintenance: thirteen energy in line with pound of body weight

For Muscle Building: 15 power in line with pound of frame weight

Eat 1 gram of protein regular with one pound of body weight.

Consuming greater than this is not vital and could no longer purpose greater muscle benefit.

Take 1-2 grams of carbohydrates constant with pound of frame weight.

The fatter you are and the greater aggressive you're looking to lose fat, the fewer carbs you need to eat.

The leaner you are the extra duration you're seeking to gain and the greater carbs you may eat. You can start with a maximum of two grams and while you acquire to 3 grams regular with body weight and need greater energy, begin such as fat.

For top-rated feature add round zero.Four grams of fat consistent with kilos bodyweight. When you have got out of place sufficient fat, you pass lower than that.

Eat 2-three Meals a Day

Research had demonstrated that it's the quantity of carbohydrates, fat, and protein that you have taken for the day that actually subjects and now not the entire amount of food which you have taken in. Hence, it doesn't absolutely rely if you eat 5-6 food a day. But eating that manner may be a hassle in particular at the same time as you are education. Cut your eating to two-three instances a day so long as you eat first-class meals based totally mostly on advocated food plan for bodybuilding. Be positive to take carbohydrate each day. Eating often has a terrible impact on testosterone degree and digestion.

Best Time to Taking Carbs

The high-quality instances of the day to have your carbohydrate diploma stuffed is round your wearing sports and at within the night. As you are education for building muscle corporations and electricity, you need carbohydrates, as they're the notable unmarried fuel for this exercising. 60-ninety minutes in advance than operating out, your meal need to at the least have 25-50 grams of carbohydrates from both of the subsequent:

A small sweet potato

A small bowl of oatmeal

A fist-length a part of white rice

Chapter 18: Best Training Exercises With Optimal Effects At Less Time

Often instances, human beings ask, "What is the super weight schooling workout for muscle constructing and strength?"

The way to that hasn't changed due to the truth then. Doing the basics are although the exceptional. To decide the effectiveness of an workout, first, it have to be an motion or a movement that allows the fine amount of loading for the muscle organisation. Second, it need to permit exquisite strength profits and development. For the identical cause, squats are better than leg extensions and army presses are higher that lateral raises. You can use greater weights on squats and navy presses and might pass as a exceptional deal as hundreds of kilos on them. Like on lateral will increase, you can begin with 10's and as you circulate more potent, you can pass up to twenty-five's some years later.

One detail you need to be aware, despite the fact that, big compound physical games can be volatile if you do them with a incredible deal a good deal much less than great shape or when you have any pre-modern damage, which could save you you from doing them properly. To make all sports solid as possible, do a little warmth ups, use bands and chains, use slower negatives and pauses. You may additionally additionally moreover add a few vicinity of expertise bars like trap bar, safety squat bar, and Swiss bar.

Here are a few primary sporting events, which you may do, in a public gymnasium.

Standing Press

As you're standing up, draw close the bar or a couple of dumbbells and bring them overhead. This will efficaciously percent some duration for your shoulders. However, make sure to compress your abs on the identical time as doing this, then pull lower lower back your ribs down as you squeeze your butt's muscle tightly in some unspecified time in the future of as you do the set. Make sure that your feet are settled firmly at the ground or floor.

Do this for 3-5 heavy gadgets as soon as in every week for electricity and 3-five better reps back off devices for size.

Clean & Press

This is the most crucial of the antique-faculty exercise. You can try this thru choosing a weight off the floor and placing it overhead. This is the essence of weight training. However, a barbell can do harm in your wrist and elbows in case your technique isn't right. So, for an smooth one, you could do easy and presses with dumbbells as an opportunity.

If you could workout the use of 50 kilos of dumbbells for a sturdy set of 10-12 reps, that is quite practicable for an prolonged-time period goal. By doing this, you could make bigger some quite large traps and big shoulders. A assume pinnacle once more and shoulder girdle also are big while using this.

Hang Clean

When you see Olympic lifters having large traps, it's due to cleans. However, they are not the maximum steady exercise nor clean to look at. But if you could do them perfectly, you will be gaining a few excessive length. It can take some time to have a observe the proper method and building up muscle organizations very, very slowly.

Farmers Walk

A muscle-constructing exercising requires wearing a few issue heavy. A farmer's stroll is finished thru choosing up multiple dumbbells or kettlebells and stroll at the same time as carrying them for about 30 seconds to 2 minutes. By doing the farmer's exercise, you're sure to boom large forearms. This exercise moreover enables p.C. Length on the traps and all the way down your lower lower back, glutes, and calves.

Most people find out the farmers walk extra powerful than any form of calf increase for along with length to the lower leg muscle tissue. One can expand stability within the ankle and knee using this exercising.

Barbell/Dumbbell Press (Flat & Incline)

The flat barbell bench press is not usually surely useful until you may do it with a reverse band installation or chains or when you have an angle or impartial grip bar. This workout can be traumatic on the shoulders. But if you may do it flawlessly, it's a nice exercise.

A 15-30 degree incline press with an angled grip barbell is ideal for constructing the chest. An45 stages incline is all proper for a selection sometimes that attitude locations extra strain on the shoulders.

Rather than have a straight away bar that hard for you, dumbbells are more steady and a more effective choice. The use of dumbbells allows your joints to move freely in a extra in reality. This will lower your restoration time among His will lower your restoration time among workout exercises and works to decorate your everyday sturdiness. In the absence of dumbbells, you could use kettlebells. If you don't have a bench, a floor press is a fantastic opportunity.

Arm Dumbbell Row

The Arm Dumbbell Row is remarkable for building up top once more and laterals. You can do it via a sawing movement to permit the burden to go with the flow in advance slightly at the lowest of each rep then pull it upward within the route of the hip.

Most men can't experience their another time or lateral muscular tissues running. This is because of the purpose that they have got a bent to go too heavy on rows. If you fail to maintain it even for at least a 2nd assume the pinnacle, then it's too heavy. Therefore, you want to lighten the burden through the use of focusing on those muscle tissue. Squeeze them hard as you can via the set to efficaciously assist bring together your decrease back muscle tissues and laterals.

Another variation of doing this exercise is a chest supported dumbbell row. Lay with face down at the bench at the same time as keeping the dumbbells. This is strong for humans with decrease lower back injuries.

Deadlift

This is a simple motion – bending over and selecting up a heavy object. This is a splendid way to paintings along with your neck, shoulders, traps, laterals, glutes, mid over again, decrease again, quads, hamstrings, center, and forearms.

Powerlifter does the deadlift plenty, which money owed for his or her massive traps and backs.

The conventional deadlift with a immediately bar from the floor is certainly one choice. You also can skip sumo or pull from pins or blocks. To beautify the start of the pull you can stand on a low discipline or some plates.

Another variation is the lure bar deadlift which has a whole lot a great deal less of a reading curve. When you begin your pull, make which you are tight from head to foot. You then take the slack out of the bar and flatten your decrease decrease returned. Your pinnacle again want to be barely rounded. To do the proper function, just unfold your shoulder blades on the equal time as maintaining your decrease back flat. Stick with low reps and construct amount thru greater units. As the reps are delivered, the threat of damage additionally increases.

Squat

The squat is considered the king of carrying activities. Squats are essentials if you are aiming to be sturdy otherwise you want to have massive legs. Don't restrict yourself on lower returned squats. Front squats are higher to your shape. For more comfort and luxury, carry out a hint squatting with a protection bar.

To make certain protection whilst doing squats, spend the preferred time to expand the vital mobility to squat nicely. Doing this will now not be interesting or a laugh but it's certain not to harm you. It is likewise actually beneficial to apply an splendid pair of Olympic lifting footwear.

Make high quality to stretch and skip your ankles, hip, calves, hamstrings, glutes, and thoracic backbone for best and damage-free squat. Also, use a load you may dominate with ideal shape. If you pass too heavy and allow the form to lighten up, you're asking for an harm.

Sled Dragging/ Pushing

Using weights even as you operate a sled is one of the amazing weight training physical video games. It can assist assemble leg period and electricity power whilst enhancing your situation on the equal time. Consider sled dragging/pushing as an important part of any schooling software.

Looking at the quads of a bicycle owner or tempo skater, you may be aware that quads respond well to extent and the high-quality part of the sled is the dearth of eccentric factor. You can pile at the amount and frequency, that allows you to make your legs extend while not having your potential to get higher getting crushed.

Standing Hammer Curl

You might not want to have large legs and torso with thin hands. The reputation hammer curl is first-class for thickening up the higher fingers and forearms. Focus in your fingers doing the art work and not on your shoulders and reduce again. You do that by means of the usage of way of compacting the weight at the pinnacle for a 2d earlier than decreasing below control for approximately three seconds. Make advantageous which you increase your elbows ninety nine percent of the manner to the lowest then without delay contrary the motion with a powerful contraction of the biceps. However, DO NOT SWING!

Chapter 19: What You Need To Know About Getting Fit Earlier Than Starting Out

To many, the concept of constructing a lean and appealing body speedy appears too farfetched. While, positive, its miles right to have realistic expectations, it's also real that with the proper attitudinal and realistic method, you may honestly build a lean and suit frame fast. However, as implied above, you want a trade of mind-set in addition to a realistic approach to the possibility.

First, earlier than you get started out on something, you need to determine in which you're at this precise second. Do you have got were given a big quantity of extra fat or are you definitely seeking to tone up and improve the advent of unique regions of your frame? The method to this query may be very essential because in the long run, your vicinity to start shall determine lots. For example, it shall determine the education technique you operate as well as the eating regimen you adopt as you bypass approximately the threat.

If you're in particular overweight, to tone up and gather a strong, lean, and attractive body, you can need to lose the greater fats overlaying your lean muscle agencies. Losing weight isn't always easy, advantageous, but no longer no longer feasible. If you are extraordinarily overweight, you could need to take a look at your food regimen and way of life choices. Essentially, to burn a pound of fat every week, you can want to reduce your weekly calorie consumption with the resource of 3500 energy, which equals 500 energy in keeping with day.

For instance, if you are a median sized woman—or depending in your calorific goals—who have to consume 2000 electricity every day to keep your frame, you may need to put off 500 electricity out of your weight-reduction plan. You can do this in ways: with the useful aid of mission bodily sports that burn 500 energy, or with the resource of way of reducing your weight loss program such which you have a caloric deficit of 500 electricity. For better effects, go with the former after which tweak your weight-reduction plan through way of inclusive of healthful meals to it. That is the primary thing you want to do.

The special component you need to do is are in search of recommendation out of your doctor. Here, especially test your body fat content material fabric cloth. The fatter you are (that means the extra fats you've got were given at diverse components of your body), the greater hard you may need to construct an appealing physique. In this equal line of concept, we cannot fail to mention which you ought to get your medical doctor to test your modern-day fitness repute. This could be very critical because of the reality what you analyze from this inquiry will dictate most of what you do and the technique you're taking as you are seeking out to assemble a lean frame.

For instance, do you have were given any shape of harm that might doubtlessly keep you from carrying out some types of bodily games? For example, when you have a back hassle, you want to exercising severe warning on the equal time as undertaking once more-sculpting bodily sports activities which include the useless enhance or barbell rows.

A Precursor: Eating Right

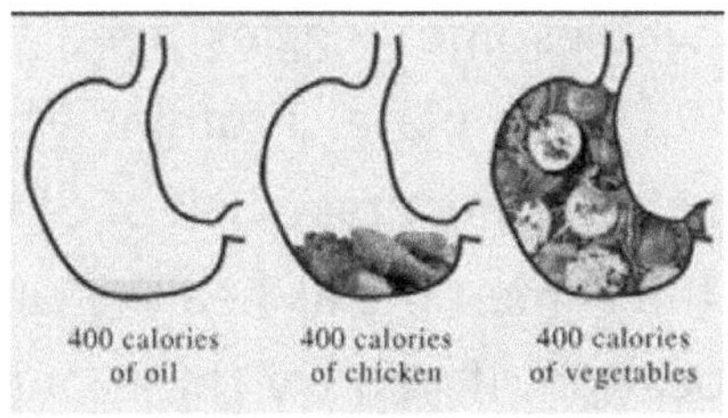

The other element, and this is of maximum importance, is to study your weight-reduction plan with the bespectacled eyes of a nutritionist. If you hold in mind not a few component from this manual, permit it is this: calories are specific; nothing illustrates this better than the photograph under.

As you can see from the photo above, the kinds of materials you consume in huge aspect decide how full you experience. If you have got been struggling with binge consuming or cravings as you're trying to find to shed pounds, bear in thoughts the styles of factors you are consuming. Here, and in most instances of thumb as regards to weight reduction and physcial fitness, eat filling elements, which as you can bet, approach extra greens. Keep the subsequent in thoughts: wholesome veggies need to make up 1/2 of of your plate. Proteins—healthful proteins at that—must take half of of the final vicinity at the same time as healthy carbs take the final location. If you try this, your weight reduction journey will seem nearly effortless.

Ideally, health thru workout additionally comes with an equal, complimentary element of diet regime. Depending in your place to begin, tweak your eating regimen therefore. If you without a doubt want to tone up, eat greater vegetables and proteins than carbs— even wholesome ones. The idea proper right here is to remove all the junk, fried meals, manmade sugars, and immoderate salt.

This guide shall no longer ask you to end up a fanatical calorie counter. With that stated, you need to be in detail aware about what you feed your frame due to the truth at the cease of the day, it gives another time what you offer it. If you devour extra veggies and slight your protein and carbs intake—hold in thoughts that greens also have a wholesome quantity of healthful carbs and fiber—you may be properly for your manner to a wholesome, lean, and sturdy frame, that is the prerequisite for an appealing frame.

Now that we've got that during thoughts, permit's get right to it. Below are the severa property you need to do to art work your manner up to an attractive body:

Chapter 20: Strength Training For A Leaner, Stronger, And Sexier Body

"No pain no advantage" is some factor you have got were given probable heard earlier than or visible plastered everywhere in the gymnasium. This analogy is one of the truest there may be: you can not chain your self to a table all day or consume plenty of burgers and count on to "sit down and eat" your manner into an appealing frame; that handiest takes place in Alice in Wonderland kind of make notion.

To get that strong, lean, and appealing body you've got continuously preferred, you need to art work for it. Here, operating for it way that, aside from making some sacrifices in the kitchen and food plan place, you moreover mght need to do however any other component: sweat it out at the gymnasium. This may be very important.

Whether you are obese or just seeking to tone up the core, butt, legs, arms, decrease again or shoulder, you ought to, other than wearing out aerobic—cardio improves your coronary heart charge and metabolism, which permits your body burn off the fat an entire lot greater efficiently—craft an adept power education utility that sees you hitting the gymnasium at the least 3 instances each week. If your three-way couple right eating regimen, aerobic, and electricity schooling, you'll get in your desired attractive frame faster and at the same time, shall amplify massive highbrow and bodily energy speedy.

Should Women Lift Heavy?

Unfortunately, and that is a few aspect you are in all likelihood to have a have a look at any time you go to your neighborhood fitness center, ladies have bought into the myth that power schooling equals a manly body, but the reality is that it isn't.

When you visit the health club, you are probable to peer lots of ladies who should instead die than increase a few component heavier than a red dumbbell, with the concern being that lifting heavier weights will translate right right into a linebacker's frame. Well, here is a punchline that you observed coming from 10 miles away: lifting heavier, whilst completed right especially with the aid of way of a woman, does no longer need to motive a "manly—for lack of a higher word—'frame'. In fact, we will exit on a limb proper right here and say that in case you carry heavier and with the perfect quantity of depth, with the proper portions of weight, you may mould a horny magazine frame that will become the envy of various ladies.

What does this let you know?

It have to tell you that you want to swim against the cutting-edge-day. Never be afraid to educate with heavier weight—in reality make certain that as you do, you're following a truely perfect power-training plan geared in the direction of "cutting" in desire to massive muscle growth; in the long run, your intention isn't to—until it's miles—become a professional frame builder.

Dismiss, right this case, the parable that lifting heavier approach becoming large and bulkier because it does not. On the contrary, in case you want an attractive body that is going outside and inside and bulges at all of the right places, snob that crimson dumbbell and as an opportunity, do compound wearing activities—the use of heavier weights—whose of entirety recruits more muscle mass.

A Strength Training Plan for Women

The concept here is straightforward: use the proper sporting sports—compound sports activities—and the proper quantities of weights—heavier weights—and if you are constant, every guarantee within the ebook is which you shall enlarge a competition worth frame this is the envy of the network.

In this subsection, we're going to carry out a touch issue simple: define the carrying occasions you want to interact in, divided with the resource of the one of a kind areas of the frame, to mildew a body that lights up your smile every time you get out of the shower or bathtub and take a look at out the mirror. Obviously, the wearing activities we can talk right here are what we called compound moves that engage more muscle groups:

NOTE: Because that may be a short take a look at, we will now not detail a way to perform the sporting sports. Instead, each exercise has a hyperlink to a video showing you the manner to carry out the exercising- all you want to do is to click on on at the name. Still on this, do 6 reps of each exercising for 4 gadgets— of path this doesn't recommend you need to do those sports activities every day. Dedicate an afternoon of the week to each of the areas mentioned beneath. For extra effects, workout each center area two times in step with week. For instance, you could have interaction in a lower body workout two instances every week.

Chapter 21: Sample Workout Plans

As implied earlier, you could choose out among splits: overall frame exercise or better/decrease split. Here, we shall outline more than one each splits bodily activities so that all you need to do is pick, create a without a doubt perfect exercising regular—consider that the idea is to educate at least three times every week—after which get to paintings (you, simply, want to paintings for it: a fantastic body comes with its honest percent of tough artwork)

1: High Intensity Total Body Workout

6 reps of (four reps)

Barbell Deadlifts

Dumbbell bench press

One arm dumbbell row

Rest for 6 seconds between sets:

2: Low Intensity Total Body Workout

12 reps of (three gadgets)

Barbell squats

Pushups

Chin-ups

Rest for 75 seconds between units

three: Upper/Lower Split (Day 1)

6 reps of (4 gadgets)

Barbell squats

Barbell deadlifts

Split Squats

Plank (3 units of however masses you could with relaxation of 30 seconds among)

four: Upper/Lower Split (Day 2)

10 reps of (three units)

Pushups

Seated cable rows (12 reps, three gadgets)

Dumbbell shoulder press (eight reps for 3 gadgets)

Chin up (10 reps for three gadgets)

Day three and four of the higher/lower cut up—day three for lower and day four for top—should consist of various carrying sports of various reps and devices. With that said, what we've got were given cited here should help you word what you want to be doing to build a lean and horny body. As implied earlier, this guide has centered on compound sports activities that once finished constantly, will provide you with the quickest effects. If there are particular areas you would love to motive along side the underarms, shoulders, and the middle, you may throw a few focused exercising into your workout recurring. However, maintain the training simple—DO NOT overcomplicate it—and use one-of-a-type intensity—regularly growth the intensity each week or bi-weekly—as well as reps and sets.

With what now, you may be nicely in your manner to a higher body.

We can not fail to commit a straightforward portion of this guide to discussing dieting in depth because as we stated earlier, what you eat shall determine what your frame gives you. If you use the know-how in this guide nicely however maintain feeding junk on your frame, all you may be doing may be for naught.

Even despite the fact that we stated food in advance, let us delve a chunk deeper into it and flesh out how you can couple what you've got observed above approximately workout with proper weight loss plan just so on the cease of four weeks—or whichever time body you have got were given selected—you may test out the replicate with a smile due to the fact the outcomes of your difficult work mirror lower back:

Nutrition and Supplementation for a Bangin' Body

"Diet" is a phrase many dread, that is comprehensible due to the reality our understanding of eating regimen usually method deprivation, i.E. To weight loss plan way you have to sacrifice and stop ingesting a number of your favorite ingredients.

However, weight loss plan and food regimen are not awful. In fact, at its truest center, weight-reduction plan in reality technique the meals you devour. Therefore, your healthy dietweight-reduction plan is the food you consume, which as we have were given got stated generally, what you consume can each help or derail your fitness and frame goals.

Unlike maximum weight-reduction plan books, this guide shall not try to shove a particular consuming plan down your throat because of the reality in the end, your frame is precise and due to it, no person ingesting plan can suit all because of the reality your body shape and metabolic charge is tremendous—due to this that what works for Mary shall not be simply right for you and vice versa. You, consequently, want to recognize how your frame works—that is why inside the first phase of this guide requested you to seek advice from your scientific health practitioner—similarly for your nutritional desires and necessities.

About Calories, BMR, and TEE

We cited power earlier. Here, we will nice element out that they may be the electricity you get from meals and that the frame makes use of to strength all bodily skills at the side of breathing, digestion, taking walks, and others—a number of which might be automated. Foods provide your frame with one in all a type macronutrients that decide the form of energy in all and sundry meals. We have 3 maximum essential macronutrients: carbohydrates, proteins, and fats.

To stay, you need a particular, easy style of electricity. This is what we all the BMR (base metabolic rate). Your base BMR is based upon on factors at the side of your lean muscle tissue, activity degree, and the likes. Your TEE (popular power expenditure) is your BMR plus the more energy your frame desires to strength activities together with workout, taking walks, napping, and the likes.

When it comes to eating regimen—weight-reduction plan is not a horrific phrase that need to conjure photographs of celery and the likes— for a bangin' frame, you want to endure in mind that macronutrients bear in mind amount hundreds. You need to eat:

Proteins

Eat enough protein due to the reality proteins are the constructing blocks of lean muscle tissue—and will assist you remodel your frame. Proteins ought to be a first-rate a part of your weight loss plan mainly now that electricity education is a essential part of your exercising every day.

Strength education exerts pressure in your muscular tissues and reasons fiber damage— this is proper and is how muscle agencies develop. Adding protein on your diet will make certain that the body uses the amino acids in proteins to rebuild and restore the muscle groups. The breakdown and repair of muscle tissues is what shall bring about stronger, leaner muscle tissue.

In this apprehend, the general rule is to devour 1 gram of protein for every pound of weight. For instance, in case you weigh one hundred eighty pounds, you want to goal to consume one hundred 80 grams of protein. As you shed kilos and construct leaner muscle groups, you can upload the quantity of protein you devour (to shred your body—get that attractive contour you have got always desired—because research has validated that in terms of shredding, improved protein intake allows). Because you can not eat this an entire lot protein in a single meal, you need to unfold it throughout splendid meal. Keep in mind that traditional proteins have 4 energy according to gram.